BRANCH LINES AROUND SHEERNESS

Vic Mitchell and Keith Smith

 Middleton Press

ISBN 1 873 793 16 2

First published July 1993

Design - Deborah Goodridge
Typesetting - Barbara Mitchell

Published by Middleton Press
Easebourne Lane
Midhurst
West Sussex
GU29 9AZ
Tel: (0730) 813169
(From 16 April 1995 - (01730) 813169)

Printed & bound by Biddles Ltd,
Guildford and Kings Lynn

CONTENTS

INDEX

MAPS

ACKNOWLEDGEMENTS

We are grateful to so many of the photographers mentioned in the captions for additional help received and also for the help given by R.M.Casserley, G.Croughton, T.Heavyside, P.Horne, N.Langridge, A.Ll. Lambert, V.Martin, J.Miller, A.Neale, M.Parker, D.Salter, P.Shaw, G.T.V.Stacey, N.Stanyon and our ever supportive wives.

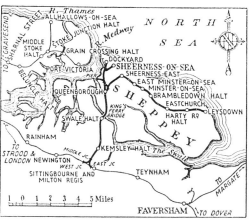

(Railway Magazine)

GEOGRAPHICAL SETTING

Sittingbourne is situated on the northern limit of the dip slope of the Chalk of the North Downs. The first part of the branch traverses the sands of the Thanet Beds as far as Kemsley, thereafter being predominantly on the Alluvium of the Thames estuary in which the Isle of Sheppey is situated. The island is separated from the mainland by The Swale, on the southern bank of which an extensive paper works developed on account of good rail and water transport.

Queenborough and the Sheppey Light Railway were built on London Clay, which was of economic importance for a pottery industry.

Being at the mouth of the River Medway, Sheerness was of strategic importance and a Naval dockyard was established there. The town grew around this and subsequently developed a holiday industry on a limited scale. The combined populations of Sheerness and nearby Minster grew from 16000 in 1861 to 22000 in 1921, by which time the railway monopoly of transport had ended.

All maps are to the scale of 25" to 1 mile unless otherwise shown.

HISTORICAL BACKGROUND

The Chatham-Faversham line was opened through Sittingbourne on 25th January 1858 by the East Kent Railway, which changed its name in the following year to the London, Chatham and Dover Railway.

The Sittingbourne & Sheerness Railway received its Act on 7th July 1856, this authorising the construction of a line to Sheerness Dockyard (opened on 19th July 1860) and a branch to a pier near Queenborough (opened to goods in about 1863 and to passengers on 15th May 1876). The main line connection faced Sittingbourne until about 1864 when a triangular junction was laid down. The S&SR was absorbed by the LCDR in 1876, although the latter had operated all trains from the outset.

While the terminus at Sheerness was conveniently situated for the Dockyard, it was remote from the town centre and so a trailing branch to "Sheerness-on-Sea" was opened on 1st June 1883 - see adjacent 1" scale map. Owing to the advent of World War I, this station was closed on 8th November 1914 but when it reopened, on 2nd January 1922, a direct connection to Sittingbourne was provided and Sheerness Dockyard was closed to passengers.

The Sheppey Light Railway was constructed under the 1896 Light Railways Act and was opened from Queenborough to Leysdown on 1st August 1901. It was operated by the South Eastern & Chatham Railway, the name used by the managing committee which controlled the LCDR and the rival South Eastern Railway from 1899 until 1923, when the Southern Railway came into being. The SECR acquired the line in 1905. Nationalisation in 1948 resulted in the lines becoming part of the Southern Region of British Railways. Complete closure of the Leysdown branch followed on 4th January 1950.

Passenger services to Sheerness were electrified on 15th June 1959. Freight service changes in the area are detailed elsewhere in this volume.

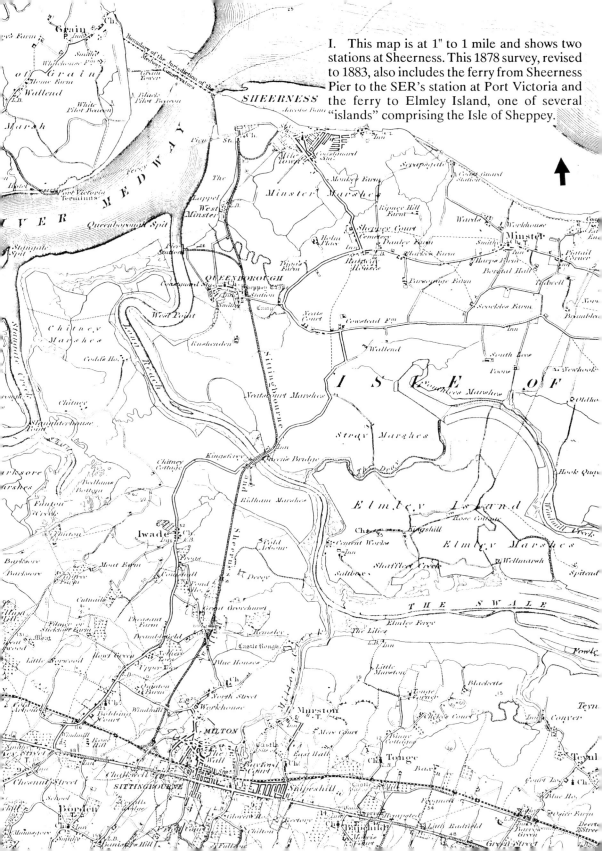

I. This map is at 1" to 1 mile and shows two stations at Sheerness. This 1878 survey, revised to 1883, also includes the ferry from Sheerness Pier to the SER's station at Port Victoria and the ferry to Elmley Island, one of several "islands" comprising the Isle of Sheppey.

PASSENGER SERVICES

These notes refer to down trains running at least five days per week, the table indicating the number of trains each day. Boat trains are excluded.

Sittingbourne to Sheerness

		Weekdays	Sundays
July	1860	5	5
June	1869	10	8
Feb.	1890	9	3
July	1906	9	7
July	1914	13	7
July	1917	8	5
July	1921	16	6
July	1924	18	10
Aug.	1928	23	14
Aug.	1934	24	17
Dec.	1938	25	13
June	1944	25	11
June	1948	23	11
June	1954	20	11

There was a considerable seasonal fluctuation in Sunday service frequency. For many decades there were additional trains direct from London on Monday mornings, typically at 6.30 from Holborn Viaduct and 6.35 from Victoria, the latter terminating at Sheerness Dockyard when both stations were open. Until WWI there were up to two trains daily direct from Chatham or beyond but by the mid-1930s there were up to five.

The 1924 timetable showed a curiosity - a 1.2am departure from Sittingbourne on the first and third Thursdays of the month.

The full electric timetable from November 1959 gave dramatic increase in frequency with three departures per hour - one to Victoria, one to Sittingbourne and one all stations to Dover Priory. This lavish provision was reduced in 1968 when the hourly Dover service was withdrawn.

Hourly operation from Victoria ended in May 1973, a half-hourly branch service being maintained until June 1981. The final direct London link finished on 2nd October 1989 when the 08.00 Sheerness to Victoria and the 17.27 Holborn Viaduct to Sheerness were withdrawn, leaving only a basic hourly branch service, with some extras in peak hours.

In May 1993 a half-hourly service was restored on weekdays. This was partly financed by the local authorities as a means of reducing the chronic traffic congestion on the only road to Sheerness. Kemsley and Swale became request stops and the overall journey time was reduced by 5-7 minutes.

Queenborough to Leysdown

The first timetables showed four trains daily but the Sunday service was soon reduced to two and in the first few winters these trains terminated at Eastchurch.

Weekday frequency was gradually increased to seven by 1908 but from the beginning of WWI to the advent of WWII, this figure was six in most years. On Sundays there were generally four trains in summer months, with two in the winter. There was an extra evening journey on Wednesdays and Saturdays during much of this period.

WWII brought three trips daily but this soon became four, weekdays only, a timetable that was perpetuated until closure.

Table 23				QUEENBOROUGH and LEYSDOWN—Third class only														
Miles	**Down**		**Week Days only**								Miles	**Up**		**Week Days only**				
		a.m	a.m	a.m		p.m							a.m	a.m	a.m		p.m		
	Queenborough ..... dep	6 30	8 16	1055	..	4 22	..	..	..	..		Leysdown .... dep	7 15	9 5	1136	..	5 5	..
1½	Sheerness East	6 35	8 21	11 0	..	4 27	..	..	..	..	1½	Harty Road Halt.......	7 20	9 10	1141	..	5 10	..
2½	East Minster-on-Sea ...	6 42	8 27	11 6	..	4 33	..	..	..	..	3½	Eastchurch............	7 25	9 15	1146	..	5 15	..
3½	Minster-on-Sea	6 45	8 31	1110	..	4 37	..	..	..	..	4½	Brambledown Halt.....	7 30	9 20	1151	..	5 20	..
4½	Brambledown Halt	6 50	8 35	1114	..	4 41	..	..	..	..	5½	Minster-on-Sea	7 34	9 24	1155	..	5 24	..
5½	Eastchurch............	6 57	8 41	1119	..	4 47	..	..	..	..	6½	East Minster-on-Sea....	7 37	9 27	1158	..	5 27	..
7	Harty Road Halt........	7 3	8 45	1124	..	4 52	..	..	..	..	7½	Sheerness East	7 44	9 34	12 5	..	5 34	..
8½	Leysdown.......... arr	7 9	8 52	1130	..	4 57	..	..	..	..	8½	Queenborough .... arr	7 49	9 39	1210	..	5 39	..

1. Branch line to Sheerness   SITTINGBOURNE

1. Approaching platform 3 on 22nd October 1921 is the 2.5pm from Sheerness Dockyard, headed by ex-LCDR class M2 no.641. The 1874 proposal for a third track to the junction has never been implemented. (K.Nunn/LCGB)

2. The station had an overall roof between about 1863 and 1952. There had been a subway near the centre of the picture and a refreshment room on the up platform (right). The station featured in the news on 31st August 1878 as five died in a collision between a Ramsgate-London express and badly shunted wagons. (Lens of Sutton)

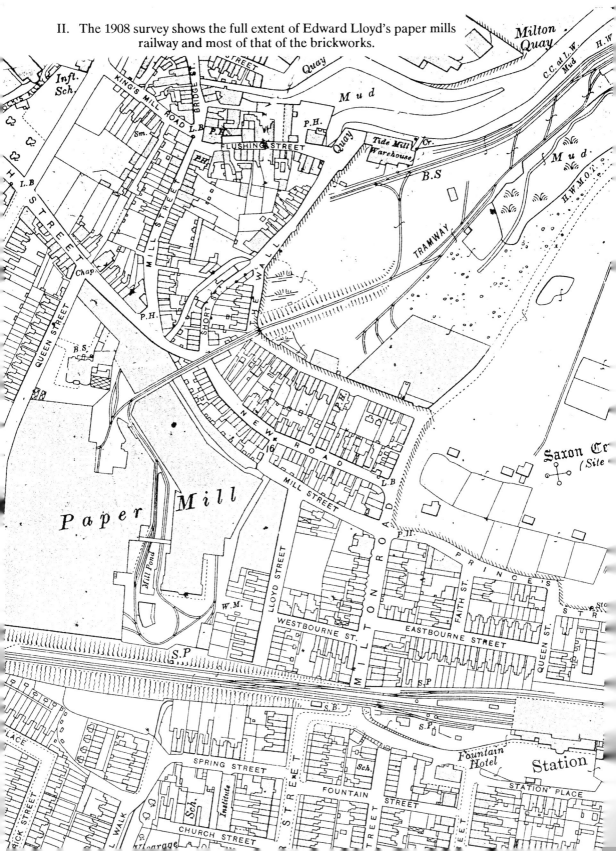

Milton Quay

Infi. Sch.

KING'S MILL ROAD

FLUSHING STREET

Quay

Mud

Quay

Tide Mill Warehouse

Mud

B.S

TRAMWAY

H.W.M.O.T.

Chap.

QUEEN STREET

SHORT ST.

MILL STREET

THE WALL

Saxon Cr (Site

Paper Mill

Mill Pond

NEW ROAD

MILL STREET

P.H.

LLOYD STREET

MILTON ROAD

PRINCE'S ST

FAITH ST.

QUEEN ST.

W.M.

WESTBOURNE ST.

EASTBOURNE STREET

S.P.

S.P.

S.P.

S.B.

Fountain Hotel

Station

SPRING STREET

Sch.

Institute

FOUNTAIN STREET

STATION PLACE

CHURCH STREET

Mud

Wharf

H.W.M.O.T.

W h a r f

Mud

C

.15

B r i c k **W o r k s**

TRAMWAY

C R O W N
Q U A Y

Post

Bronze Weapons
found A.D. 1824

Allot.
Gdns.

L A N E

P.H.

L.B

C R O W N

SOUTH EASTERN & CHATHAM RAILWAY

TRAMWAY

S.P.

Goods
Shed

Cr.

S.B.

S.P.

S.P.

Swimming
Bath

Workman's

rsery

21

3. Most Sheerness branch trains have used the down loop and platform 3. Class B2 0-6-0 no.654 waits to depart on 13th March 1926, its presence not having enhanced the washing set out to dry in the adjacent garden. The locomotive was one of a class of six built for the LCDR by the Vulcan Foundry.
(H.C.Casserley)

4. This view from the 1950s includes the fully enclosed footbridge, the new platform canopies and the gentlemen's accommodation, originally unroofed. Changes since the previous picture include upper quadrant signals, Sugg's gas lamps and flat bottom rails.
(H.C.Casserley coll.)

5.   All change in 1959. Seen on 18th May is class 2 2-6-2T no.41311, only a few days before electrification. The lighting is also being electrified, and the platforms extended and raised. Colour light signalling, controlled from a new signal box, was introduced on 24th May 1959. (A.E.Bennett)

For other views of this station and its goods yard please see the companion album *Sittingbourne to Ramsgate*.

6.   The historic building, seen in 1980, remained little changed in 1993. The small canopy is in the place of a large bay window - both canopies have since been replaced by a long narrow glazed structure, renovation being completed in December 1986. (N.D.Mundy)

7. A westward view on 7th September 1988, from the then unglazed footbridge, includes the 10.12 from Sheerness and covered sidings used for unloading tankers of china clay and chalk slurry for the Sittingbourne Paper Company's mill which dominates the scene. (J.Scrace)

8. Unit no.1614 has just arrived at platform 3 after working the 12.36 from Sheerness on 14th August 1992. No.47309 is hauling the 05.22 Willesden-Sheerness freight, the leading wagon of which contains liquid oxygen for use in steel making. (J.Scrace)

SITTINGBOURNE JUNCTIONS

III. The London to Sittingbourne line runs from top left (Western Junction) to bottom right (Eastern Junction). Top right is the Sheerness branch and Middle Junction. This 1908 edition includes Lowe's siding, lower right.

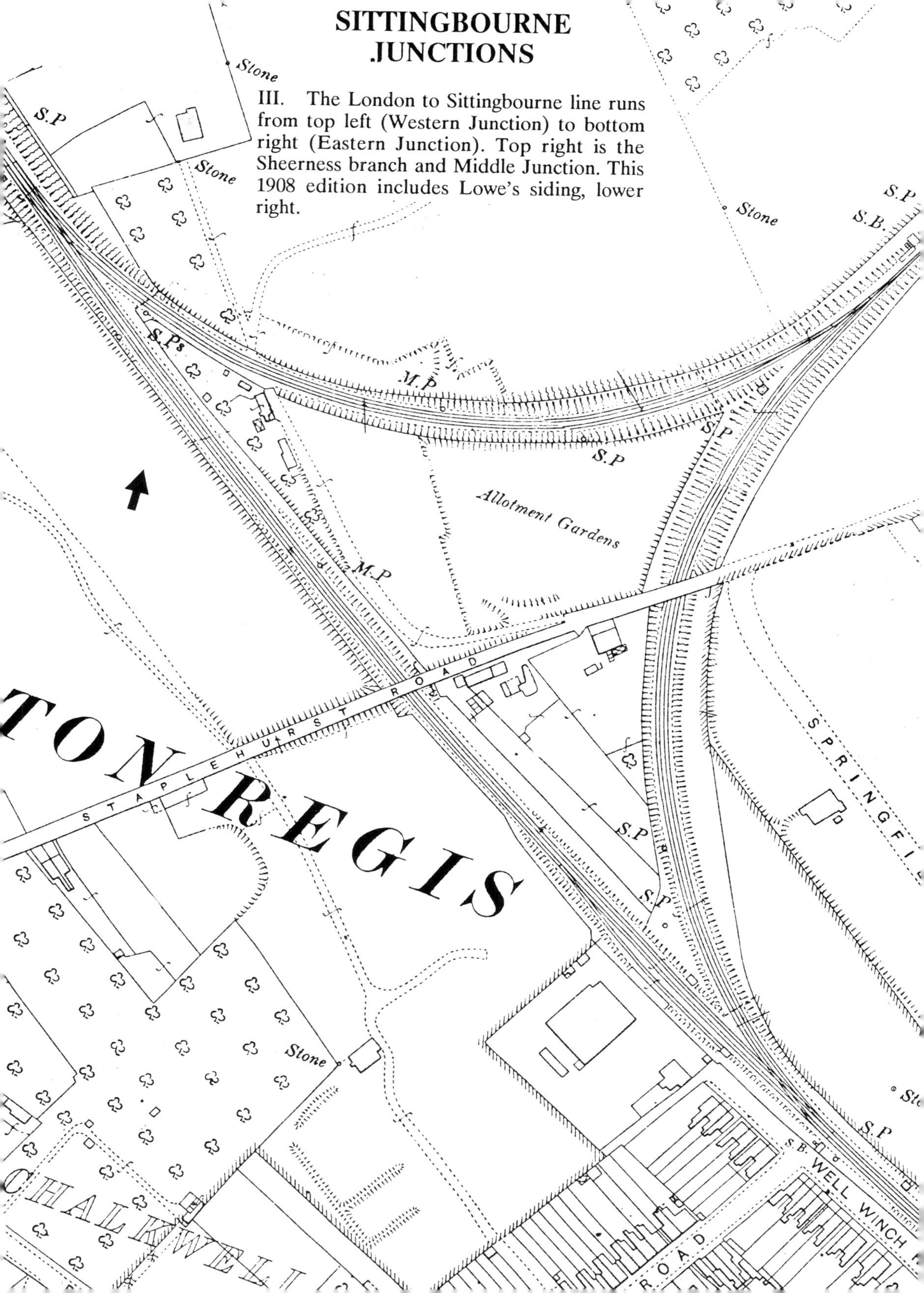

Stone

S.P

Stone

Stone

S.P

S.B.

S.P.

M.P

S.P

Allotment Gardens

S.P

M.P

STAPLEHURST ROAD

TON REGIS

SPRINGFI

S.P.

S.P.

Stone

S.P

Sto

CHALKWELL

S.B. WELL WINCH

ROAD

9. Sittingbourne Western Junction is seen in April 1950, the lines to Sheerness being on the left. The signal box was replaced by a new one on 10th May 1953, this being abolished on 24th May 1959. (Pamlin Prints)

10. A locomotive and two vans approach Sittingbourne Eastern Junction from the branch on 23rd May 1959. A signal box is marked on the map but it was closed on 26th November 1933, the junction being worked from Sittingbourne "A" Box from that time until the introduction of colour light signalling. (J.J.Smith)

11. The signals seen in the previous picture were nearing the end of their working days when recorded in 1958, by which time conductor rails were lying in the "four-foot" awaiting installation. (N.W.Sprinks)

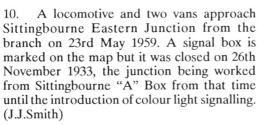

12.   A northward view in 1950 shows the double tracks on both sides of the triangular junctions merging onto the single track of the branch line to Sheerness. The featureless landscape of the Isle of Sheppey is in the background. (D.Cullum)

13.   Middle Junction Box is seen on a brighter day in September 1954. Note the platform for exchanging single line tokens, the window cleaning balcony and the Tilley lamp above it. (J.J.Smith)

14. Middle Junction up distants are evident in these two 1958 photographs which feature work in progress on the preparations for doubling of the track north to Swale Bridge, prior to electrification. The bridge illustrated here is in the background of the previous picture. (N.W.Sprinks)

15. LMS designed 2-6-2T no.41309 displays a clean emblem as it hauls two BR Mk.I corridor sets, separated by an elderly ex-SECR compartment coach. The signals are of even greater antiquity. (N.W.Sprinks)

KEMSLEY

16. Kemsley Halt was opened on 1st January 1927 and comprised a single wooden platform. It served a new housing development and paper mills. Class D 4-4-0 no.1729 is bound for Sittingbourne. (D.Cullum coll.)

IV. The 1938 map marks the loop and second platform which came into use on 26th June of that year. The provision of this loop reduced the headway from eleven to six minutes.

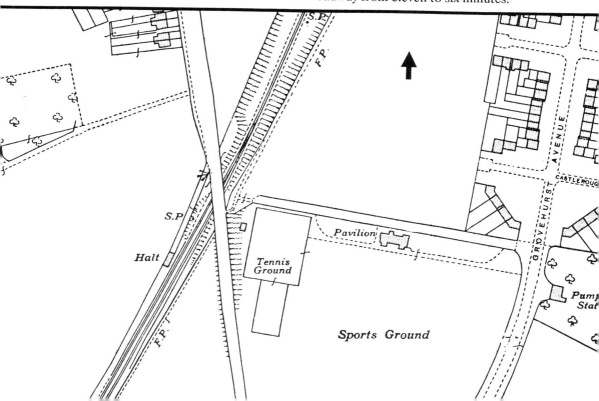

17.   Class 2 2-6-2T no.41313 is working the 12.40pm Sheerness to Chatham direct service on 22nd June 1957. The signalling lever frame was situated in the booking office, seen at the far end of the down platform. An up bracket signal beyond the bridge enabled up trains to use the down loop when the signal box was switched out at quiet times. (J.H.Aston)

18.   No.47234 is operating a Speedlink service on 19th July 1990. It is the 13.53 Sheerness to Glasgow Mossend, which was devoted principally to imported Japanese cars. The footbridge was added prior to electrification in 1959 but by 1990 the shelters for passengers had vanished. (J.Scrace)

RIDHAM DOCK

V. Construction of the dock started in 1913 but its completion was hindered by the advent of WWI and the Royal Navy using the facilities for disposal of equipment during 1919-21. Thereafter the dock was used for its intended purpose, which was mainly the landing of timber and fuel for the nearby paper mills. Standard and narrow gauge tracks were provided, the latter being illustrated in this volume in pictures 23 to 34. This is the 1939 survey, reduced to 20" to 1 mile. The aerial ropeway was used for the conveyance of timber from ship to mill, as the railway could not cope with all the traffic.

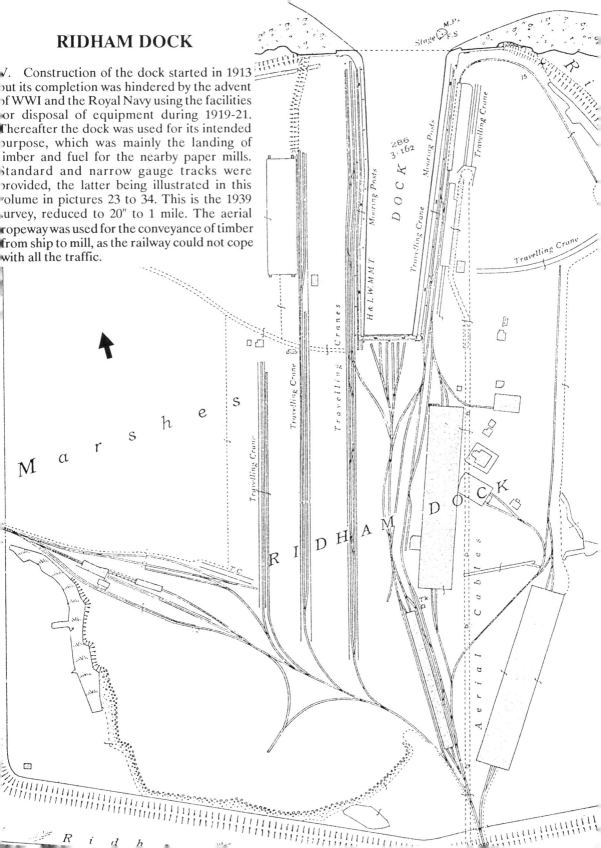

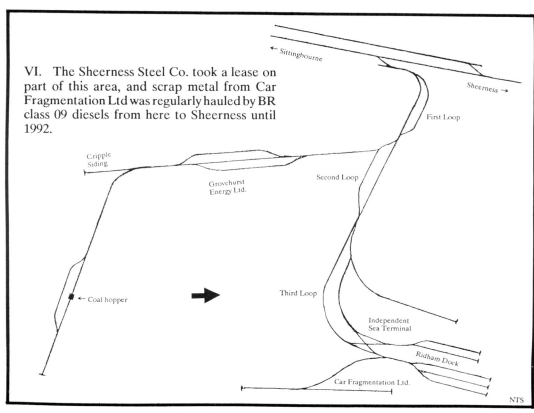

VI. The Sheerness Steel Co. took a lease on part of this area, and scrap metal from Car Fragmentation Ltd was regularly hauled by BR class 09 diesels from here to Sheerness until 1992.

← Sittingbourne

Sheerness →

First Loop

Cripple Siding

Grovehurst Energy Ltd.

Second Loop

Coal hopper →

Third Loop

Independent Sea Terminal

Ridham Dock

Car Fragmentation Ltd.

NTS

19. The Ridham Dock siding diverges from the branch between Kemsley and The Swale Bridge, visible in the distance. The Hunslet of Grovehurst Energy Ltd waits in First Loop on 15th April 1993. (V.Mitchell)

20. The cranes of Ridham Dock are in the background as no.73005 waits at Second Loop on 15th October 1979. On the right is class 08 no.157, by then owned by Sheerness Steel who used part of the site for scrap iron processing. (R.E.Ruffell)

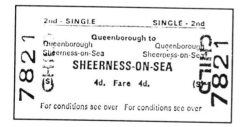

21. In connection with use of part of the dock in 1919, the Admiralty obtained two locomotives. A 2ft 6ins gauge Kerr Stuart 0-4-2T of their "Skylark" class (no.802 of 1904 and often wrongly recorded as named *Skylark*) accompanied by a 4-4-2T from the LSWR. The former was regauged and sold to the Snailbeach District Railway and the latter went to the East Kent Light Railway, the engineer to both lines being Colonel H.F.Stephens. No.488 is now to be found on the Bluebell Railway, its unusual life history being outlined in our *Branch Line to Lyme Regis*. (R.L.Ratcliffe coll.)

2. Bowater's Railway

VII. The paper mill of Edward Lloyds Ltd was built close to Sittingbourne station but most of its raw materials were sea-borne, via Milton Creek. A 2ft 6ins gauge tramway was laid between the wharf and the mill, the route being shown in detail on map II. The line was horse worked until three 0-4-2 STs were bought from Kerr Stuart & Co. in 1908. To gain access to deeper water the company constructed Ridham Dock (top right) and greatly extended the railway. As already mentioned, work commenced in 1913 but the dock was requisitioned by the Admiralty in 1917 and retained for four years, being used latterly for shipbreaking. A new mill at Kemsley (centre) was completed in 1924 and connected to the rail network which was by then 10 miles in total, the main line being 3½ miles in length. The firm was acquired by the Bowater Group in 1948.

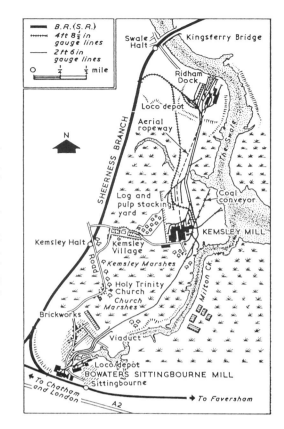

22. For shunting their standard gauge sidings, Bowaters acquired P class no.31178 from BR in 1958. Named by them *Pioneer II*, it is seen on 4th October 1969, along with one of its two Drewry diesel companions, prior to acquisition by the Bluebell Railway where it is still located. (S.C.Nash)

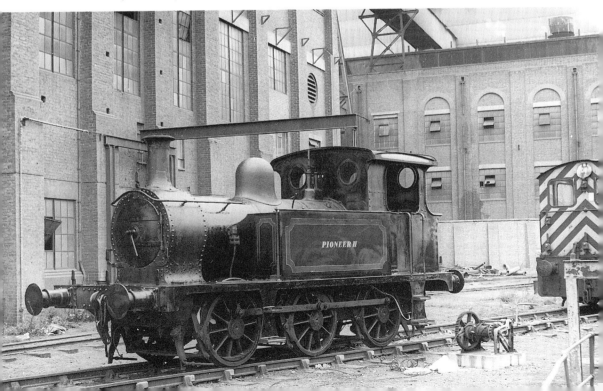

23.   The reason for fitting a spark arresting chimney is evident as 0-6-2T *Conqueror* shunts bales of waste paper on 1st March 1968. Loose paper on the ground was the greatest potential hazard, particularly in dry weather. (A.G.Thorpe)

24.   Four 0-4-2 STs were obtained from Kerr Stuart & Co between 1904 and 1924, this example being seen at the Ridham Dock shed on 14th May 1960. These locomotives were used mainly for shunting, whereas the six 0-6-2Ts were employed on the long haul to the mills. (R.C.Riley)

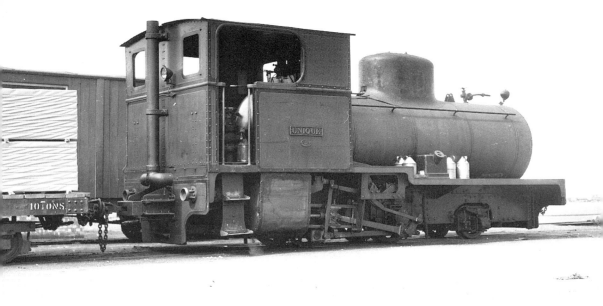

25.   Seen on the same day is one of the company's two fireless locomotives, steam for which was obtained periodically from the works supply via a hose. The exhaust pipe is on the rear of the cab. This is *Unique*; the other was *Victor*, an 0-4-0. Both were built by Bagnall and *Unique* was put on static display at Kemsley after its retirement. (R.C.Riley)

26.   A new locomotive depot was completed at Kemsley in 1954, the last in Britain on a commercial narrow gauge system. The well equipped premises were photographed on 15th June 1957, along with the 1934-built Bagnall, *Triumph*. (S.C.Nash)

27. *Superior* was the only Kerr Stuart 0-6-2T in the fleet and was recorded on a coal train in June 1957. The other non-Bagnall 0-6-2T was *Chevallier*, this emanating from Manning Wardle in 1915. Also in a class of its own was the 0-4-4-0 *Monarch*, provided by Bagnall in 1953. (J.H.Aston)

TIME TABLE of GOODS TRAINS for FLUSHING SERVICE.

WEEK DAYS.

These Trains must take precedence over all other Goods Trains, which must be shunted for them.

Mr. Willes at Loughboro' Sorting Sidings must telegraph daily to Sittingbourne the time of departure of the down Train, that the staff working may be arranged at Middle Junction.

UP.	Week-days only. No. 1.		Week-days only. No. 2.				DOWN.	Not on Mons. No. 1. A		Not on Sats. No. 2. B			
	arr. p.m.	dep. p.m.	arr. a.m.	dep. a.m.				arr. a.m.	dep. a.m.	arr. p.m.	dep. p.m.		
Sheerness	...	8 30	...	...	...	...	Stewart's Lane	...	...	...	8 50	...	...
Queenboro'	8 35	9 10	...	...	...	...	Blackfriars	...	3 45	...	...	...	...
Queenboro' Pier	9 15	10 15	...	3 0	...	...	Herne Hill Sidings	4 0	4 30	9 3	9 40	...	...
Queenboro'	10 20	10 30	3 4	3 5	...	...	Herne Hill	pass	4 32	9 0	9 45	...	...
Middle Junction	10 46	10 47	3 17	3 18	...	...	Beckenham	...	4 50	...	10 1	...	...
Western Junction pass	...	10 50	...	3 19	...	...	Swanley	pass	5 19	10 36	10 45	...	...
New Brompton ... pass	...	11 15	...	3 34	...	...	Farningham	...	...	10 55	11 10	...	...
Chatham	11 22	11 27	...	3 37	...	...	Chatham Goods Sidgs.	6 9	6 25	...	11 47	...	...
Chatham Sidings	11 32	11 55	...	3 40	...	...	Chatham	pass	6 28	...	11 50	...	...
Swanley	...	12 50	...	4 20	...	...	New Brompton	6 36	6 55	...	11 55	...	...
Beckenham .... pass	...	1 15	...	4 40	...	...	Western Junction pass	...	7 21	...	...	...	...
Herne Hill	1 32	1 37	...	4 53	...	...	Eastern Junction	...	...	...	...	...	...
Herne Hill Sidings	1 40	1 50	...	4 55	...	...	Sittingbourne	...	...	12 10	12 40	...	...
Blackfriars	2 0	...	5 5	...	...	...	Eastern Junction	...	...	...	...	...	...
Stewart's Lane	...	...	...	...	...	...	Middle Junction	7 23	7 24	12 42	12 42	...	...
							Queenboro'	7 42	7 52	12 55	1 15	...	...
							Sheerness	7 57	...	...	...	...	...
							Queenboro'	...	...	...	...	...	...
							Queenboro' Pier	...	...	1 20	...	...	...
							Queenboro'	...	...	...	...	...	...
							Sheerness	...	...	...	...	...	...

July 1888

28. The southern part of the route was carried on a concrete viaduct nearly a half mile in length. A train of paper bales and workers' coaches is approaching Sittingbourne on 11th August 1954. Five new coaches were bought in 1958 and 13 passenger trains were run throughout the 24 hours of each day. (H.C.Casserley)

29. In addition to *Pioneer II* and two 0-6-0 diesels, Bowaters had *Jubilee* on their standard gauge tracks for many years. It was built by Bagnall in 1936. (J.J.Smith)

30. Closure of the narrow gauge line was inevitable but the company was reluctant to see the system disappear totally and arranged to lease the Kemsley - Sittingbourne section to the Locomotive Club of Great Britain. Here we witness *Triumph* leaving Ridham Dock for the transfer ceremony on 4th October 1969. (S.C.Nash)

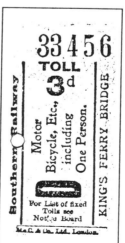

3. Sittingbourne and Kemsley Light Railway

31. A passenger terminus was built at Kemsley Down and public services commenced on 28th March 1970, mostly operated at weekends, but not in the winter. The terminus is viewed on 20th October 1973, the engine shed road being in the foreground. There is no road access to this station. (E.Wilmshurst)

32. A new engine shed was erected at Kemsley Down, as the railway had to be fenced off from the paper mill. Kerr Stuart 0-4-2ST *Melior* is in residence on 29th August 1992. (P.G.Barnes)

33. The Sittingbourne terminus was photographed on 23rd October 1971, with 0-6-2T *Superb* waiting to leave. The indigenous coaches were supplemented by four from the Chattenden & Upnor Railway, a Naval line on the western shore of the Medway Estuary, north of Chatham. (E.Wilmshurst)

34. After nearly 60 years of service the half-mile long concrete viaduct was deemed unfit for further traffic due to severe spalling. For the 1993 season a station was opened near the public rubbish tip in Gas Lane, and a former Bowaters coach was provided as a booking office. The 0-6-2T *Triumph* is returning the coaches to the platform of Milton Halt on 10th April 1993, having had the assistance of a diesel to shunt from the other end of the train. (V.Mitchell)

Branch Line to Sheerness - continued
SWALE

35. The halt south of the bridge was in public use from 1923 and was named King's Ferry Halt until becoming Swale Halt in 1929. The simple structure is seen from the main road in 1957. (J.H.Aston)

VIII. The 1939 map indicates that the main road to Sheerness passes under the railway south of Swale Halt.

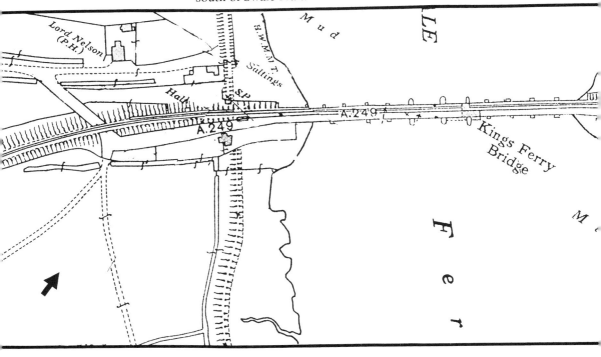

KING'S FERRY BRIDGE HALTS

Notes by D.W.Winkworth

The first halt (which is designated 1) was opened on 23rd November 1913 for the use of Messrs. Thomas Oliver and Son's workmen. This contractor was building a wharf and extension of premises for Messrs Edward Lloyd Ltd on land abutting on the south side of The Swale. The SECR agreed to put in a goods siding, for the delivery of construction materials situated between Middle Junction and Swale Bridge. This junction still exists as the junction to Ridham Dock. The 200 feet long halt was situated on the main line, rather than on the siding, possibly immediately south of the junction, and was used solely by Oliver's workmen. This halt was shown in the railway's working timetable but not in the public timetable. The contract was expected to last 18 months but, in a supplement to the working timetable dated 1st October 1914, the note concerning Oliver's workmen changes to Trollope & Colls' workmen. These arrangements were included in the working timetables of 1915 and 1916 but not 1917, suggesting the work had been completed during 1916 and that the halt was no longer used.

In 1917 the Admiralty had established a General Salvage Depot at Ridham and the working timetable dated 1st January 1918 had workmens trains (the service possibly started during the previous November) running from Sittingbourne to Ridham Dock, the SECR locomotive being exchanged for the dock locomotive at the junction. As from 1st May 1918 some other trains to/from Sheerness were booked to call at Kings Ferry Bridge Halt. By 14th June 1920 the service to Ridham Dock had disappeared from the timetables, the depot having, presumably, closed in 1919 or early 1920 but other trains were still calling at Kings Ferry Bridge Halt and continued to do so in 1921 and 1922.

On 17th December 1922, the Kings Ferry bridge was heavily damaged when a ship collided with it whilst trying to pass through and road and rail communication was completely severed, recourse having to be made to small boats to ferry people across. At first train passengers had to use ladders to get to and from the trains working up to the gap but very quickly the railway company built two temporary halts, one each side of the bridge, both being known as Kings Ferry Bridge Halt (for this purpose the one on the south side is designated 2 and that to the north 3). These halts were commissioned certainly by New Year's Day 1923. From 1st March 1923, passengers were able to walk over the bridge, instead of using ferries. A handbill issued on 25th September 1923 indicated all trains serving the emergency halts (2 and 3) and some trains the original (1) halt. This was possibly the first occasion that the original halt had been advertised to the general public. On 1st November 1923 the through rail service was restored and two of the halts immediately closed, one of which was that north of the bridge (3) and the other south of the bridge. But which one south of the bridge is not known. One of these continued to be used because it was included in both working and public timetables until the issue of 3rd March 1929 when the name was changed to Swale Halt. The original (1) halt could have closed as from 1st November 1923 or it could have gone on for a period.

Dates for the opening of Swale Halt in the location (2) by the bridge are often quoted as June or July, but both the SR timetable and Bradshaw include it in their issues of 3rd March 1929 and a local timetable published by the East Kent Gazette in its 20th April 1929 issue includes it as such.

REVISION OF TRAIN SERVICE.

MONDAY, OCTOBER 1st, 1923, and until further notice.

In consequence of the repairs to the King's Ferry Bridge not being completed, the Train Service will be as shown below, (instead of as shown in Time Tables dated October 1st), until further notice:—

DOWN TRAINS—Week-days.

		a.m	a.m	a.m	a.m	a.m	a.m	a.m	a.m	p.m	S.O.	N.S.	S.O.	S.O.	p.m	N.S.	S.O.	p.m	p.m
Sittingbourne ...	dep	5 35	6 19	7 23	8 0	8 57	9 47	10 40	11†21	12 20	1 25	1 58	2 5	2 55	3 40	4 23	4 35	5 10	6 0
King's Ferry Bdge. Halt	arr.	5 44	6 28	...	...	...	...	...	...	...	...	...	...	...	...	...	...	...	...
A King's Ferry Bdge.	arr	5 47	6 32	7 33	8 10	9 7	9 57	10 50	11†31	12 30	1 35	2 8	2 15	3 5	3 50	4 35	4 48	5 20	6 10
A King's Ferry Bdge.	dep	6 7	6 47	7 43	8 25	9 17	10 12	11 6	11 50	12 46	1 45	2 18	2 20	3 15	4 0	4 45	4 55	5 35	6 25
Queenborough ...	arr	6 12	6 52	7 48	8 30	9 22	10 17	11 10	11 54	12 51	1 50	2 23	2 25	3 20	4 5	4 50	5 0	5 40	6 30
Queenborough ...	dep	6 17	6 54	7 50	8 32	9 27	10 19	11 12	12 0	12 53	1 52	2 25	2 27	3 22	4 10	4 51	5 1	5 42	6 35
Sheerness-on-Sea	arr	6 23	7 0	7 56	8 38	9 33	10 25	11 18	12 6	12 59	1 58	2 34	2 43	3 26	4 16	4 57	5 7	5 45	6 41

DOWN TRAINS—Week Days—cont.

		p.m	p.m	p.m	p.m
Sittingbourne ...	dep	7 3	8 10	9 10	9 50
King's Ferry Bdge. Halt	arr.	...	...	...	...
A King's Ferry Bdge.	arr	7 13	8 20	9 20	10 0
A King's Ferry Bdge.	dep	7 30	8 35	9 35	10 15
Queenborough ...	arr	7 35	8 40	9 40	10 20
Queenborough ...	dep	7 37	8 42	9 42	10 22
Sheerness-on-Sea	arr	7 43	8 48	9 48	10 28

DOWN TRAINS—Sundays.

		a.m	a.m	p.m	p.m	p.m	p.m	p.m	p.m
Sittingbourne ..	dep.	9 15	10 50	2 35	3 27	5 35	8 5	8 55	9 35
A King's Ferry Bdge.	arr.	9 25	11 0	2 45	3 37	5 45	8 15	9 5	9 45
A King's Ferry Bdge.	dep.	9 40	11 15	3 0	3 50	6 7	8 20	9 15	9 55
Queenborough ..	arr.	9 45	11 20	3 5	3 55	6 12	8 35	9 20	10 0
Queenborough ..	dep.	9 47	11 22	3 7	3 57	6 17	8 37	9 22	10 2
Sheerness-on-Sea ..	arr.	9 53	11 28	3 13	4 3	6 23	8 43	9 28	10 8

UP TRAINS—Week-days.

		a.m	a.m	a.m	a.m	a.m	a.m	a.m	a.m	p.m	S.O.	N.S.	S.O.	S.O.	p.m	N.S.	S.O	N.S.
Sheerness-on-Sea	dep	5 25	6 30	7 10	8 4	8 55	9 47	10 32	11 25	12 15	1 20	1 55	2 5	2 50	3 35	4 23	4 30	5 2
Queenborough ...	arr	5 30	6 35	7 15	8 9	9 0	9 52	10 37	11 30	12 20	1 25	2 0	2 10	2 55	3 40	4 28	4 35	5 7
Queenborough ...	dep	5 31	6 37	7 17	8 11	9 2	9 54	10 39	11 32	12 22	1 27	2 2	2 12	2 57	3 42	4 29	4 37	5 8
A King's Ferry Bdge.	arr	5 36	6 42	7 23	8 16	9 7	9 59	10 44	11 38	12 28	1 32	2 7	2 17	3 2	3 47	4 34	4 42	5 13
A King's Ferry Bdge.	dep	5 54	6 57	7 38	8 31	9 17	10 14	10 57	11 53	12 43	1 45	2 17	2 25	3 15	4 5	4 45	4 55	5 26
King's Ferry Bdge. Halt	dep.	...	...	...	...	...	...	...	...	...	...	...	...	...	...	...	...	5 29
Sittingbourne ...	arr	6 †7	7 7	7 48	8 41	9 25	10 24	11 7	12 3	12 53	1 55	2 25	2 38	3 25	4 13	4 55	5 5	5 36

UP TRAINS—Week Days—continued.

		S.O.	p.m	p.m	p.m	p.m	p.m
Sheerness-on-Sea	dep	5 15	6 5	6 55	8 15	9 0	9 55
Queenborough ...	arr	5 20	6 10	7 0	8 20	9 5	10 0
Queenborough ...	dep	5 22	6 12	7 2	8 22	9 7	10 2
A King's Ferry Bdge	arr	5 27	6 17	7 7	8 27	9 12	10 7
A King's Ferry Bdge.	dep	5 35	6 32	7 22	8 42	9 25	10 17
King's Ferry Bdge. Halt	dep.	...	...	...	...	...	...
Sittingbourne ...	arr	5 45	6 42	7 30	8 52	9 33	10 27

UP TRAINS—Sundays.

		a.m	a.m	a.m	p.m	p.m	p.m	p.m	p.m	p.m
Sheerness-on-S.	dep.	6 30	9 0	10 55	1 35	3 20	4 47	[illegible]	8 55	9 35
Queenborough	arr.	6 35	9 5	11 0	1 57	3 25	4 52	4 13	9 0	9 40
Queenborough	dep.	6 37	9 7	11 2	1 59	3 27	4 55	[illegible]	9 2	9 42
A King's Ferry B.	arr.	6 42	9 12	11 7	[illegible]	3 32	5 0	[illegible]	9 7	9 47
A King's Ferry B.	dep.	6 57	9 27	11 22	2 12	3 45	5 15	3 35	9 17	9 57
Sittingbourne ..	arr.	7 7	9 37	11 32	2 22	3 55	5 25	3 45	9 25	10 5

†—7 minutes later on Saturdays.

A—Passengers will walk the short distance between the Halt Platforms. S.O.—Saturdays only. N.S.—Not on Saturdays.

OTHER TRAIN ALTERATIONS.—WEEK-DAYS.

6.27 a.m. Sheerness to Strood, will start from Faversham at 6.40 a.m. and take up booked working from Sittingbourne at 6.55 a.m.

8.10 a.m. Strood to Sheerness will be diverted to Faversham, as under ;—

		a.m.
Sittingbourne	dep.	8 48
Teynham	,,	8 56
Faversham	arr.	9 3

2.45 p.m. (N.S.) }
3. 5 p.m. (S.O.) } Charing Cross to Sheerness, will terminate at Sittingbourne.

7.8 p.m. (N.S.) Cannon Street }
6.56 p.m. (S.O.) Charing Cross } to Sheerness will be diverted to Faversham via Sittingbourne, as under.—

	p.m. arr.	p.m. dep.
Sittingbourne	9 0	9 2
Faversham	9 14	...

7.10 p.m. Sheerness to Victoria, will start from Sittingbourne at 7.40 p.m.

10.16 p.m. Sittingbourne to Faversham, will not run.

SUNDAYS.

7. 0 p.m. Charing Cross to Sheerness will be diverted to Sittingbourne and Faversham, arriving 8.50 p.m. and 9.5 p.m. respectively.

9.53 p.m. Sheerness to Strood, will start from Faversham at 10.5 p.m.

Note that the special timetable shows three Kings Ferry Bridge Halts in use simultaneously! Only one main line engine was on the Isle of Sheppey at the time of the accident and so two P class 0-6-0Ts (nos.27 and 325) were dismantled and taken by sea from Chatham Dockyard to Sheerness Dockyard, where they were reassembled to work the island services. A direct service to London from Sheerness was provided via ferry boat to Port Victoria on the Isle of Grain, a revival of the SER's route.

Bridge closure to rail traffic

From	To	Reason
29-11-97	14-12-97	Storm damage
17-12-22	1-11-23	Bridge hit by 7000 ton *S.S. Gyp*
14-8-36	21-8-36	Bridge lowered too quickly
31-1-53	2-3-53	Flood damage to track
3-10-54	8-10-54	Bridge hit by 2112 ton *S.S. Louisa Gorthon*

36. Flat-bottomed ferry boats of about 20-ton capacity were in use until the first bridge was completed in about 1858. It was designed to carry road and rail traffic over eleven spans, the centre one opening. It was replaced by this structure in 1904, traffic commencing on 4th November. The unusual structure, which was built to an American patented design known as the Scherzer rolling-lift type, was considered to be economical to construct and maintain. (J.J.Smith)

←

Road tolls were received by the railway until 1st July 1929. These are the charges applicable in 1921.

	s. d.
For every Four-wheeled Coach or Wagon	2. 0
For every Hearse, Omnibus, Steam Engine or other four-wheeled carriage of any kind whatsoever not being a Coach or Wagon	1. 6
For every Chaise, Gig, Dog-Cart, Cart, Barrow or other two-wheeled Carriage of any kind	6
For every Motor Car under 3 tons	1. 6
For every Motor Car over 3 tons	2. 0
For every Traction Engine, threshing and other agricultural machine and for every van lorry and other vehicle carrying goods propelled by mechanical power -	
Under 3 tons	1. 6
Over 3 tons and under 5 tons	2. 0
For every ton or part of a ton over 5 tons in weight per additional	3
For every trailer to such traction engine, threshing and other agricultural machine van lorry and other vehicle -	
Under 3 tons	1. 6
Over 3 tons and under 5 tons	2. 0
For every ton or part of a ton over 5 tons in weight per ton additional	3
For every bicycle or tricycle propelled by mechanical power	3
For every trailer thereto	1
For every bicycle or tricycle not so propelled	1
For every adult person beyond the first which a bicycle or tricycle whether propelled by mechanical power or not is constructed to carry	1
For every person which a trailer to a bicycle or tricycle whether propelled by mechanical power or not is constructed to carry	1
For every omnibus or char-a-banc or other vehicle propelled by mechanical power carrying passengers	
Under 3 tons	1. 6
Over 3 tons	2. 0

SOUTHERN RAILWAY.
This ticket is issued subject to the Company's Bye-laws, Regulations and Conditions in their Time Tables, Notices and Book of Regulations.

1909

Sheerness-on-Sea to
Sheerness-on-Sea
Sittingbourne & M.R.   Sheerness-on-Sea
                        Sittingbourne & M.R.
SITTINGBOURNE   & MILTON
                 REGIS
THIRD CLASS (S.4) THIRD CLASS
Fare 1/-   Fare 1/-

1909

37. Six pictures from 1960 show the new bridge alongside the 1904 structure. Under the concrete nameboard is an afterthought - "Alight here for Ridham Dock". In 1929 Kent County Council paid the SR £50,000 for the elimination of its road toll rights, which were netting about £1500 per annum. (J.J.Smith)

38. This and the previous illustration include colour light signals mounted on temporary scaffold supports. A northbound electric train rises on the 1 in 103 gradient up to the road underbridge. The new platform is in the background. (J.J.Smith)

39. The new platform, shelter, signal and trap point are clear. Less obvious are the steps leading to the old platform and the road bridge, by now redundant. The 1929 agreement with the SR gave KCC a liability of half the cost of maintenance or replacement of the bridge. (J.J.Smith)

40. The narrowness of the road on the bridge resulted in traffic lights being installed in 1932. These were operated by the signalman, KCC paying the SR £50 per annum for the service. This is a southward view. (J.J.Smith)

41. The old bridge was opened infrequently until the development of Ridham Dock but by 1920 the span was moved an average of 150 times per month. The new lifting span weighs 465 tons and is counterbalanced by four 110 ton weights in the towers. (S.C.Nash)

QUEENBOROUGH and LEYSDOWN (One class only).—Southern.

Miles.	Down.	Week Days.							Sundays.					Up.	Week Days.						Sundays.			
		mrn	mrn	aen	aft	aft	aft	aft	X	mrn	aft	aft	aft			mrn	mrn	mrn	aft	aft	aft	X	aft	aft	aft	aft
	Queenborough ....dep.	6 45	8 18	11 0	2 10	4 10	6 45	7 20	9 45	11 20	2 55	6 10	8 10		Leysdown.............dep.	7 38	9 0	11 52	3 15	5 25	8 0	10 25	12 35	4 30	7 25	8 50
2¾	Sheerness East ...	6 51	8 23	11 52	2 15	4 17	6 50	7 25	9 50	11 25	3 0	6 15	8 15	1¾	Harty Road Halt.........	7 43	9 5	11 57	3 20	5 30	8 5	10 30	12 40	4 37	7 30	8 55
3¾	East Minster-on-Sea ...	6 55	8 27	11 2	2 19	4 22	6 54	7 29	9 54	11 29	3 4	6 20	8 19	3¾	Eastchurch.............	7 48	9 10	12 2	3 27	5 40	8 10	10 35	12 45	4 47	7 35	9 0
4¾	Minster-on-Sea...........	7 1	8 30	11 22	2 24	4 26	6 57	7 32	9 57	11 32	3 7	6 23	8 22	4¾	Brambledown Halt.......	7 54	9 16	12 8	3 33	5 46	8 16	10 41	12 51	4 52	7 42	9 6
4¾	Brambledown Halt.....7	5	8 34	11 32	2 34	4 37	7 1	7 36	10 1	11 36	3 11	6 27	8 26	5¾	Minster-on-Sea..........	7 58	9 20	12 12	3 38	5 51	8 20	10 45	12 55	4 57	7 47	9 10
5¾	Eastchurch	7 15	8 40	11 52	2 38	4 39	7 7	7 43	10 7	11 42	3 16	6 33	8 32	6¾	East Minster-on-Sea......	8 1	9 23	12 15	3 41	5 52	8 25	10 48	12 58	4 57	7 52	9 13
7¾	Harty Road Halt.......7	20	8 45	11 57	2 37	4 17	7 12	7 47	10 12	11 47	3 21	6 39	8 37	7¾	Sheerness East	8 5	9 27	12 19	3 45	6	8 30	10 52	1 2	5	7 56	9 17
8¾	Leysdown ....arr.	7 25	8 50	11 42	2 42	4 48	7 17	7 52	10 17	11 52	3 26	6 44	8 42	8¾	Queenborough 273 .....arr.	8 10	9 32	12 24	3 50	6	8 35	10 57	1	7 5	6 8	9 22

X Wednesdays and Saturdays.

1924

42. The bridge was officially opened by HRH Duchess of Kent on 20th April 1960, although trains had used it for ten days. Gas and electricity mains pass down the piers and through a tunnel under the bed of The Swale. There is no conductor rail on the 95ft. long lifting span, which takes 90 seconds to rise. The control room, the windows of which are visible, is continuously staffed. (J.J.Smith)

43. An August 1992 northward view shows the old track alignment and that the new platform can accommodate eight coaches. The bridge operator acts under the control of the Sittingbourne signalman who has a bridge release switch on his panel. (J.Scrace)

44.   A 1923 picture shows the temporary platform (3) in use on the northern shore of The Swale during the bridge closure that year. The P class 0-6-0T is one of those imported by sea to Sheppey to serve the 26,000 inhabitants isolated from the mainland at that time. (G.Metherell)

SOUTHERN RAILWAY.
Issued subject to the Bye-laws, Regulations &
Conditions in the Company's Bills and Notices.
Swale Halt   to
Swale Halt   Swale Halt
Queenborough   Queenborough
QUEENBOROUGH
THIRD CLASS   THIRD CLASS
Fare 5½d.   Fare 5½d.
NOT TRANSFERABLE.

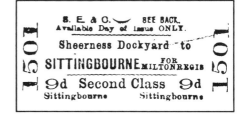

S. E. & C.   SEE BACK.
Available Day of Issue ONLY.
Sheerness Dockyard   to
SITTINGBOURNEFOR MILTON REGIS
9d   Second Class   9d
Sittingbourne   Sittingbourne

1213
S. E. & C. R. (See back
SUNDAY TICKET
Available day of issue only
Chatham (M.L.) to
QUEENBORO'
Third 1/0

45.   Queenborough is in the background as no.56038 departs on 21st October 1992 with a load of steel destined for Cardiff. It is slowing for the curve that leads on to the bridge, the 30mph speed restriction board being in the foreground. (J.S.Petley)

QUEENBOROUGH

IX. The 1908 survey at 6" to 1 mile includes the full length of the Pier Branch and marks the site of Sheppey Castle, which was built by King Edward III in the 14th century. The associated community was named after his queen. The Sittingbourne - Sheerness line runs from bottom to top and the Sheppey Light Railway is on the right. Three different tramways are also marked.

46. When the branch was opened in 1860 this was the only intermediate station, its impressive architecture being appropriate for a place with regal connections, although the local traffic must have been meagre. The footbridge (right) was built by the SECR. (Lens of Sutton)

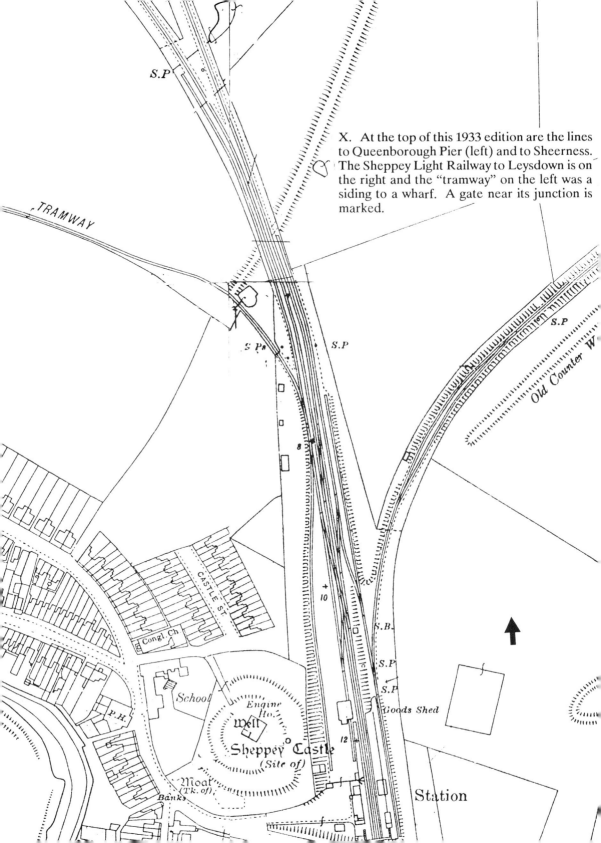

X. At the top of this 1933 edition are the lines to Queenborough Pier (left) and to Sheerness. The Sheppey Light Railway to Leysdown is on the right and the "tramway" on the left was a siding to a wharf. A gate near its junction is marked.

S.P

TRAMWAY

S.P

S.P

Old Counter W

S.P

8

+
10

CASTLE ST.

Congl. Ch.

S.B.

S.P

S.P

School

Engine
Ho.

Well

Goods Shed

P.H.

12

Sheppey Castle
(Site of)

Station

Moat
(Tk. of)

Banks

47.   A waiting shelter with canopy was provided on the up platform but no weather protection was available on the down side. Guards' look-outs and oil lamp housings dominate the roof lines, while a water tank on the castle mound makes a feature of the sky line. Under the tank was a steam pump which raised water from the castle well for railway purposes. (Lens of Sutton)

48.   The sizeable goods shed is evident, as are the signals for the Pier Branch which curved to the left in the distance. (Lens of Sutton)

49. An up goods rattles past the signal box on 4th March 1950, the signal arm for the Pier Branch having been removed. Also included in this panorama is the starting signal for Leysdown trains. No.31583 is of class C and had not yet received a BR cast numberplate on its smokebox door. (D.Cullum)

50. There were no public level crossings on the Sheerness branch but there were eleven occupation crossings and numerous foot crossings. Cyclists wait to cross one of the latter on 4th March 1950 as class H 0-4-4T no.31308 heads south. (D.Cullum)

51. The same locomotive was recorded on a grey day in December 1950 as it entered the station with the 12.10pm Sheerness to Chatham via Sittingbourne. A down train and the Leysdown train occupy the other two platforms. (J.R.W.Kirkby)

52. The 3.54pm from Sittingbourne was hauled by C class 0-6-0 no.31510 on 25th May 1958. A mobile crane stands in the yard, the goods shed crane being limited to a 35cwt. load. (S.C.Nash)

53.   Blood and custard coach livery is evident as class C no.31510 departs for Sittingbourne with the 4.25pm from Sheerness on 25th May 1958. The sidings in the foreground led to the industrial complex described in the next section. (S.C.Nash)

54.   The white patch on the bridge improved the sighting of the signal on the right of the previous picture. Class 2 no.41311 is at the end of the loop with the 5.40pm from Sheerness on 5th September 1958. (P.Hay)

55. Trains pass on the same day, the guard's periscope being visible on the roof of the nearest coach. The signal box closed on 24th May 1959; the goods shed had already gone but the yard remained open for public traffic until 16th August 1971. (P.Hay)

56. Unit 1535 is working the 16.42 from Sheerness on 19th July 1990, while woods occupy the site of the former Sheppey Light Railway. The A249 strides across the marshes and the railway on piers in the background. There is now a footway direct to the up platform from the road. (J.Scrace)

57. By 1993 most of the building was unused, the booking office being staffed on weekdays to mid-morning only. Large numbers of people travel to Sheerness from here during the day, far more than the conductor can issue with tickets. A rural ambience is maintained, despite much urbanisation of the district. (V.Mitchell)

58. Diesel shunter no.09020 waits in the up siding as electro-diesel no.73108 stands with an up freight on 5th July 1992. Shunting movements are controlled by a ground frame, electrically locked from Sittingbourne Panel. (F.Hornby)

59.   A 1992 southward view from the up
platform shows the points at the end of the
loop and the siding to Queenborough Rolling
Mill. The next map reveals the former use of
this area. (F.Hornby)

60.   Standing on the siding at the right of the
previous picture on 14th August 1992 is
no.8690, a Planet diesel owned by Queenborough Rolling Mill. (F.Hornby)

61.   A southward view from the road bridge in
1993 includes the straight line to Swale Bridge,
a large expanse of Japanese cars (beyond the
trees) and the rolling mill sidings, the first
curve leading to their locomotive shed.
(V.Mitchell)

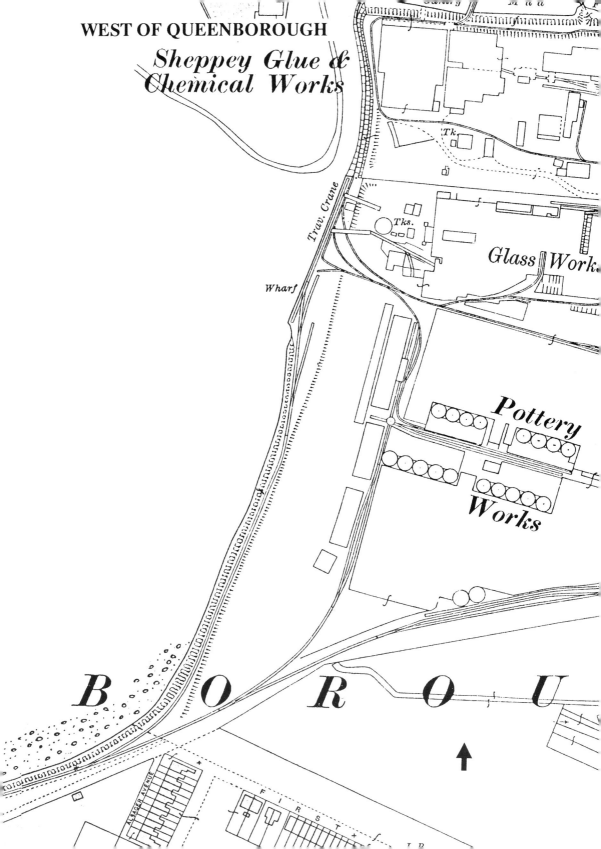

WEST OF QUEENBOROUGH

Sheppey Glue &
Chemical Works

Trav. Crane

Tk

Tks.

Glass Works.

Wharf

Pottery

Works

B   O   R   O   U

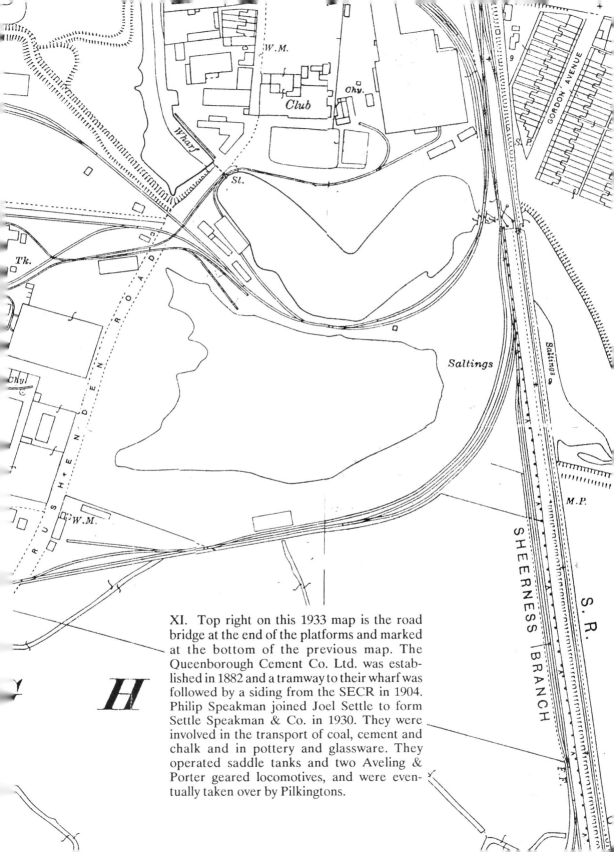

W.M.

Chy.

Club

Wharf

St.

Tk.

Chy.

W.M.

GORDON AVENUE

9

S.P.

Saltings

Saltings

M.P.

SHEERNESS BRANCH

S. R.

R U S H E N D E N   R O A D

F.P.

H

XI. Top right on this 1933 map is the road bridge at the end of the platforms and marked at the bottom of the previous map. The Queenborough Cement Co. Ltd. was established in 1882 and a tramway to their wharf was followed by a siding from the SECR in 1904. Philip Speakman joined Joel Settle to form Settle Speakman & Co. in 1930. They were involved in the transport of coal, cement and chalk and in pottery and glassware. They operated saddle tanks and two Aveling & Porter geared locomotives, and were eventually taken over by Pilkingtons.

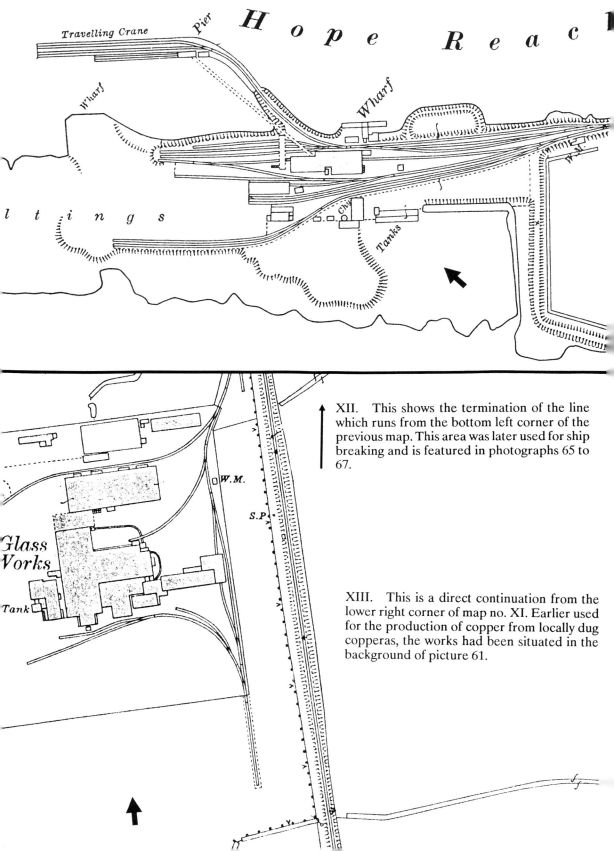

Travelling Crane   Pier   H o p e   R e a c h

Wharf   Wharf

l   t   i   n   g   s

W.M.

Tanks

XII. This shows the termination of the line which runs from the bottom left corner of the previous map. This area was later used for ship breaking and is featured in photographs 65 to 67.

W.M.

S.P.

Glass Works

Tank

XIII. This is a direct continuation from the lower right corner of map no. XI. Earlier used for the production of copper from locally dug copperas, the works had been situated in the background of picture 61.

62. Settle Speakman's geared locomotives were supplemented by this 1922 Peckett, *Johnson*, seen in front of the kilns on 28th September 1949. (A.G.Wells/Dr.E.Course)

63. This and the next four photographs were taken on 14th May 1981, when much of the former Settle Speakman site was in use by Shipbreakers (Queenborough) Ltd. This firm also dismantled rolling stock, sometimes using it briefly and at other times exporting it. No records remain of this item. (R.E.Ruffell)

64. Much ex-BR rolling stock was to be seen near the firm's engine shed which backed onto Rushden Road. The access line is shown in picture 61. (R.E.Ruffell)

65. Ex-BR property was used for everything from a mess room to the transport of scrap steel. Much of this was destined to Sheerness Steel Works, the trains first having to cross the Rushden Road level crossing before reaching BR. (R.E.Ruffell)

66. Some of the cranes installed by Settle Speakman in 1953 were still in use 40 years later, having served to break ships in the 1980s and to export re-rolled steel in the 1990s. The mill converts redundant BR rail into reinforcing rods. (R.E.Ruffell)

67. The pier had been established by 1896 and has been used for a variety of traffic over the years, including coal, chalk and steel. The BR class 03 was ideal for use on the pier, having a short wheelbase of 9ft. and weighing only 30 tons. (R.E.Ruffell)

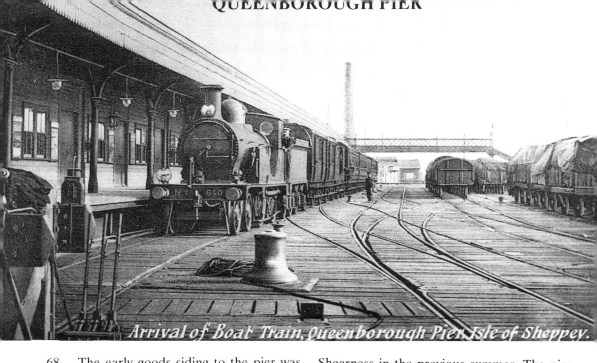

Arrival of Boat Train, Queenborough Pier Isle of Sheppey.

68. The early goods siding to the pier was upgraded and opened for boat trains to reach a new and longer pier on 15th May 1876. The Zeeland Steamship Co. operated a nightly service to Holland (Flushing - now Vlissigen) from that date, having run a trial service from Sheerness in the previous summer. The pier was closed twice due to fire damage (19-5-1882 for three weekks and 17-7-1900 for six months). A German mail service commenced on 1st June 1887. (H.C.Casserley coll.)

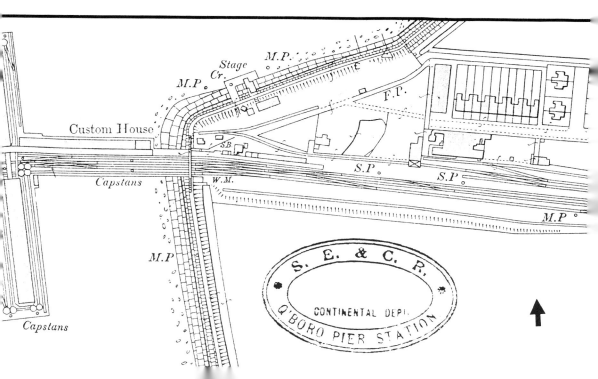

69. Passenger sailings ceased in 1916, due to
World War I, but the facilities were used for
military traffic. A signal and the signal box are
visible in this view towards the buffer stops,
which on at least one occasion prevented a
train entering The Swale. The box closed on
25th May 1934. (Lens of Sutton)

SOUTHERN RAILWAY.
Available on DAY of issue ONLY.
This ticket is issued subject to the By-laws,
Regulations and Conditions stated in the
Company's Time Tables, Bills and Notices.
Sheerness-on-Sea to
(S.9)
QUEENBOROUGH
FARE Third Class FARE
3d. 3d.
Queenborough   Queenborough

2295 2295

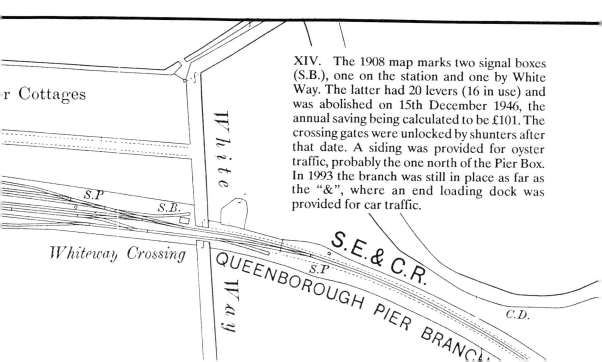

XIV. The 1908 map marks two signal boxes
(S.B.), one on the station and one by White
Way. The latter had 20 levers (16 in use) and
was abolished on 15th December 1946, the
annual saving being calculated to be £101. The
crossing gates were unlocked by shunters after
that date. A siding was provided for oyster
traffic, probably the one north of the Pier Box.
In 1993 the branch was still in place as far as
the "&", where an end loading dock was
provided for car traffic.

r Cottages

White Way

S.P.

S.B.

Whiteway Crossing

QUEENBOROUGH PIER BRANCH

S.E.& C.R.

S.P

C.D.

70. The footpath carried the coastal public footpath and was not intended for passenger use. The anticipated coal import business did not materialise and revival of passenger services after WWI was a failure. Bradshaw of 1898 announced the attraction of "lavatory coaches" on the Flushing route.
(Lens of Sutton)

Extract from the Appendix of 1934.

QUEENBOROUGH PIER.

Goods train working.— When a goods train is propelled from Queenborough Junction to Queenborough Pier, or vice versa, the person in charge at the station from which the propelling is taking place must satisfy himself that a brake van is the leading vehicle, and that a Guard fully conversant with the branch is riding therein, and is provided with a horn or whistle for the purpose of warning anyone who may be upon the line.

No train so propelled must exceed a speed of eight miles an hour.

Queenborough Pier.—The pier at Queenborough and the railway lines laid thereon are used by the Port of Queenborough Limited, and traffic for shipment by that firm is dealt with on the pier lines.

A scotch (the key of which is kept by the Station Master at Queenborough station) is provided across No. 1 siding rails immediately on the pier side of the footbridge, and this scotch must be kept locked across the rails except when wagons are being worked to and from the siding.

Whiteway Crossing box must be opened for the passage of traffic to and from the pier.

The working is under the control of the Station Master at Queenborough, who must depute a competent man to accompany each draft of wagons to and from the pier. The competent man must obtain the key of the scotch from the Station Master before leaving Queenborough.

Ingoing wagons must be placed on the siding at the south side of the pier (No. 3 siding) whence they will be worked forward by means of a capstan by the employees of the Port of Queenborough Limited. Empty wagons will be placed on the siding next to the platform road (No. 1 siding), any surplus vehicles being left on the middle road (No. 2 siding). The empty wagons must be hauled from Nos. 1 and 2 sidings to Queenborough station by the Company's engine.

Engines must not proceed on to the pier beyond the engine restriction board, which has been provided on the footbridge, at which point ingoing and outgoing wagons are exchanged.

71. For staff safety, railings were added along the platform edge, probably during the black-out restrictions of WWII when the white paint would have also been applied to the canopy stanchions. The Admiralty used the facilities prior to this photograph being taken in 1950. (D.Cullum)

72. Only the substantial stops remained of the former four-track formation when recorded in 1953. The branch had been worked as a siding since 1946. The final period of boat train operation was from 22nd December 1922 until 1st March 1923, when most traffic was concentrated on the Channel Coast ports or Harwich. The station was demolished in 1956 and is now the site of a chemical works. (N.W.Sprinks)

BLU[

St. Paul's Church

Pier Toll Ho.

PIER

L.B

School

TERMINUS ROAD

Police Station

Terminus

Wel

M u d

Reservoir
Ordnance Well House

H.W.M.O.T.

S.P

S.P.

S.P.

XV. The 1898 map shows a step in the western boundary fence ready for the proposed connection to the dockyard. The SER offered a rival and quicker service to London via Port Victoria and a free ferry from Sheerness Pier (left), this commencing on 11th September 1882. To counter this, the LCDR opened a branch (lower right) to a station nearer to the town centre. It came into use on 1st June 1883 and was named "Sheerness-on-Sea". The SER route was discontinued on 1st June 1901, following the formation of the SECR, although it was twelve miles shorter.

S.P

S.P

SHEERNESS
STATION
L.C.D.R.

Chimney

F.S

Naval Recreation Ground

73. This indifferent photograph is included as it shows the engine shed (extreme right) which was probably in use until 1905. The black fence on the left is on the alignment of the line to the dockyard, the buildings of which are in the left background. (Lens of Sutton)

74. The overall roof, seen in the previous picture and shown on the 1898 map, was largely removed and replaced by platform canopies. The trackwork is notable for its complexity and is worthy of study. (Lens of Sutton)

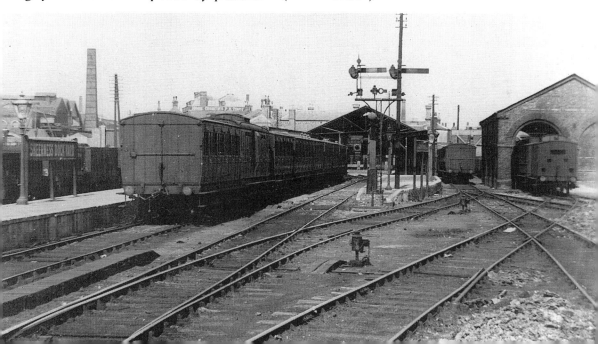

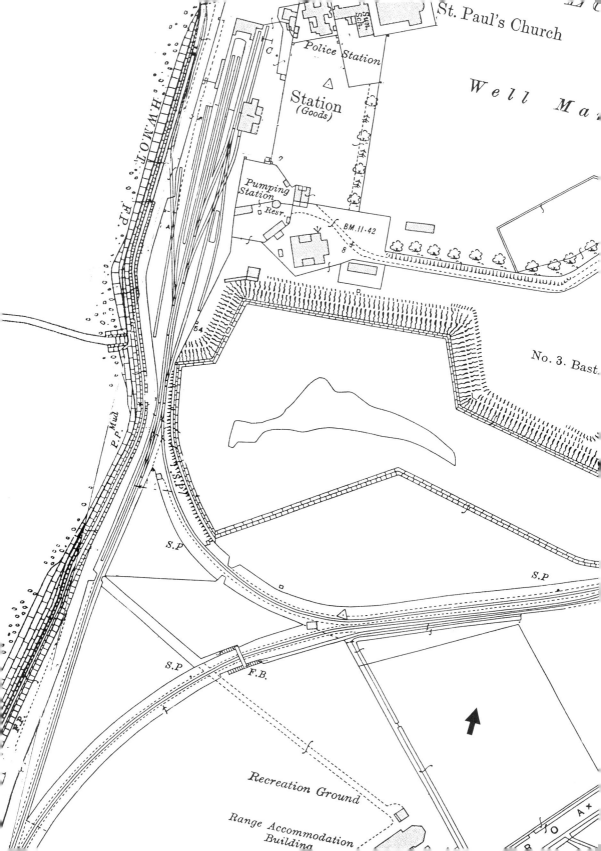

St. Paul's Church

Well Ma

Police Station

Station
(Goods)

C

Pumping
Station

Resr.

BM.11·42

8

LOWM.H.W.

F.P.

No. 3. Bast.

P.P. Mud

S.P

S.P

S.P

S.P

S.P

F.B.

F.P.

Recreation Ground

Range Accommodation
Building

TOWN

No. 2. Bastion

Raven

Terminus

THE MOAT

S.Ps.

SHORT STREET

NORTH STREET

RUSSELL

S.R. A

S.P.

S.P.

SB

BROAD STREET

HOPE

S.R.

M.P.

SHEERNESS BRANCH

BM.7.18

LB

PH

ROSE

Stone &c.

School

Infant School

XVI. The 1939 survey includes the spur from South Junction (just off the lower left corner) to East Junction (centre) which was opened on 2nd January 1922, the day on which Sheerness Dockyard (top left) became a goods station only. Sheerness-on-Sea (top right) was almost exclusively a passenger station.

MILE TOWN

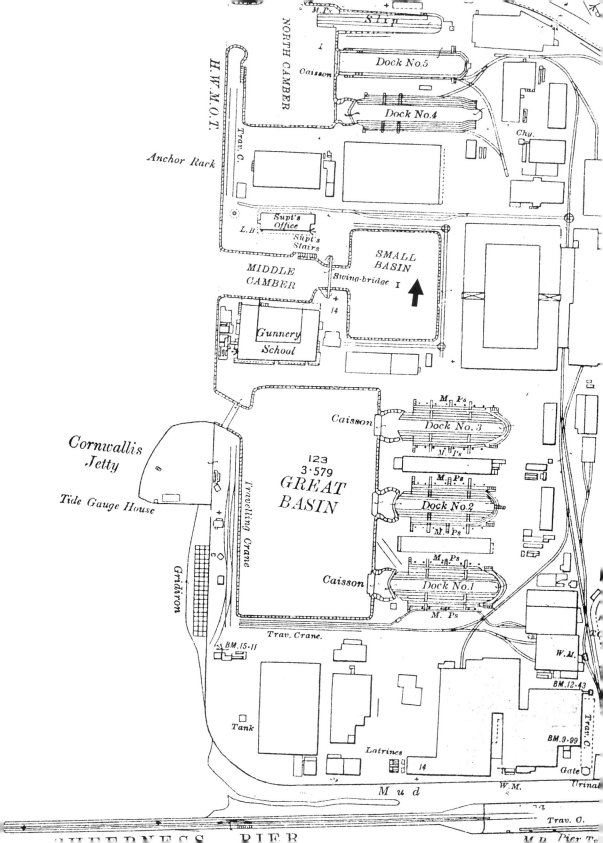

XVII. The lower right corner of this map connects with the top left corner of the previous one at the point where the Admiralty siding enters the dockyard. The connection was laid in 1902 although there had been standard gauge track in the yard since about 1870. A 2-4-0T arrived in 1872, one of two sold by the Somerset & Dorset Railway at that time.

75. A closer view of the goods shed on 16th October 1920 includes the intricate pointwork and class M1 4-4-0 no.635, a locomotive of LCDR origin. (K.Nunn/LCGB)

76. A 1922 photograph of the stops reveals that the two tracks diverged to accommodate a sector plate. This resembled a turntable but its limit of rotation was about 30 degrees. The device reduced the space required for engine release crossovers. (Lens of Sutton)

77. Class B2 no.653 was the only SECR engine on the Isle of Sheppey when the bridge was damaged on Sunday 17th December 1922 and in consequence local engines were hired. Settle Speakman provided their Peckett 0-6-0ST *Emerald Isle* (right) to work to Leysdown, but, with no continuous brakes and a proneness to axle box overheating, speed was severely limited. Sheerness Dockyard offered a Hawthorn Leslie 0-4-0ST (centre) which was used to maintain a service between Queenborough and Queenborough Pier in connection with a temporary steamer service to Port Victoria. The shed was already little used by this time. (Lens of Sutton)

78. Empty stock from Margate has just arrived on 2nd January 1957 behind class D1 4-4-0 no.31494. The suffix "Dockyard" was added when the second station opened in 1883. (J.J.Smith)

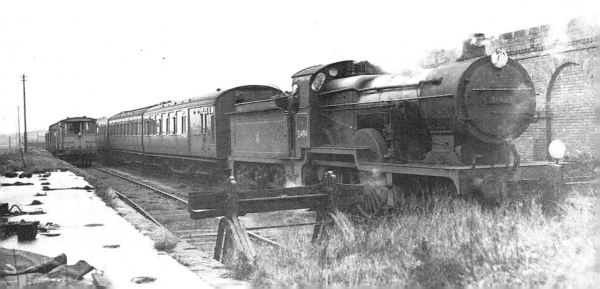

79.   Turning round we see the original terminal buildings remarkably intact. The stops probably date from the opening and are in the background of picture 76. They would have been too close together after the installation of the sector plate. (D.Cullum coll.)

80.   Windowless and unwanted, the historic structure was demolished in 1971 after 111 years. The Navy left Sheerness in 1960, goods services were withdrawn on 6th May 1963 and the remaining private siding closed on 8th March 1965, but was not officially taken out of use until October 1968. (D.Cullum coll.)

81.   Set 471 is standing on the former up platform road while vans are berthed in line with the goods shed on 26th July 1953. The coaches had formed the 11.17am Bromley South to Sheerness-on-Sea excursion that day. The gates to the dockyard line are indistinct being almost in line with the large chimney. (N.W.Sprinks)

82. In 1972 the Sheerness Steel Company commenced production on a site between the two Sheerness stations. The firm is a subsidiary of the North American Co-Steel Inc. This is almost from the same viewpoint as for picture 78 and the view includes one of the company's two class 08 shunters at work in April 1993. Rails still passed under the gate and across the road but were unused, the former Dockyard having largely become a terminal for Olau Line ferries to Vlissingen. (V.Mitchell)

83.   With the splitting signals for Sheerness
Dockyard in the background, class M1 no.635
accelerates its train of assorted six-wheelers
south on 16th October 1920. Lineside
vegetable allotments were usually only
allocated to railwaymen, owing to the lack of
fencing. (K.Nunn/LCGB)

84.   This and the next three pictures were
taken on Sunday 26th July 1953. After having
discharged the day-trippers at Sheerness-
on-Sea for a day on the beach, Q class no.30544
propels the empty excursion coaches along the
northern part of the triangular junction for
berthing in the goods sidings, as seen in picture
78. (N.W.Sprinks)

85. No.30544 is coupled behind its sister, no.30541, which had worked the 10.50am excursion from Victoria. They are facing South Junction where the ground frame would be released to enable them to travel to Gillingham for servicing, prior to working the excursions back. No.30541 is now resident on the Bluebell Railway. (N.W.Sprinks)

86. Class E no.31166 creeps along the 1922 line between South Junction and East Junction with the 12.49pm local service from Sittingbourne, comprised of one three-coach Birdcage set. The three-flight footbridge is marked on the 1939 map - lower left. (N.W.Sprinks)

87. A few minutes later, the same engine departs with the 1.30pm to Sittingbourne with a 3-car SR set of Maunsell design and a Birdcage set. The line from Sheerness Dockyard is converging on the left. (N.W.Sprinks)

88. Excursion stock is being backed from Sheerness Dockyard to Sheerness-on-Sea prior to loading holidaymakers for the trip home on 25th May 1958. On the right is the parallel line marked in the centre of the left page of map XVI. The locomotives are D1 class no.31749 and E1 no.31506. (S.C.Nash)

89. A northward view from South Junction in 1993 includes much of the Sheerness Steel Company's works and a liquid oxygen tanker standing on their departure line. This is now known as the "Westminster Straight" and was originally the main line to the terminus. The hut houses a ground frame which is released from Sittingbourne Panel. The works is on the area marked "Well Marsh" and "The Moat" on map XVI. (V.Mitchell)

90. East Junction has been moved much closer to the present Sheerness station, just visible in the distance. The catch points and foot crossing are on the BR connection to the steelwork's two reception roads, which are on the site of the former link between the two stations. The sidings in the left distance are used for loading finished steel, such as the coiled rod stacked by the building. (V.Mitchell)

91. A view in the opposite direction on 10th
April 1993 includes work in progress on a
shunter's footpath and bogie bolster wagons
standing on a reception road. On the adjacent
siding are some of Sheerness Steel's own
wagons for internal use. (V.Mitchell)

SHEERNESS-ON-SEA

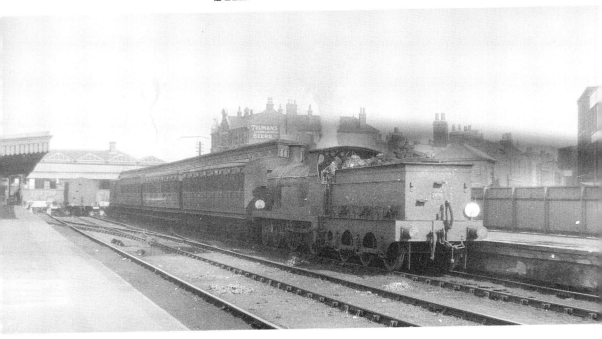

92. An SECR train stands at platform 2, giving us the opportunity to see the engine release crossovers then provided from both platform roads. These probably date from the opening of the station on 1st June 1883. The locomotive is a Stirling F1 class 4-4-0. (Lens of Sutton)

93. As a wartime economy measure, the station was closed on 8th November 1914. However, it did not reopen until 2nd January 1922, when the new direct line came into use. Class H 0-4-4T no.31308 waits to leave for Chatham on 4th March 1950. (Pamlin Prints)

94. The 3.0pm departure for Sittingbourne on 26th July 1953 was hauled by an ex-SECR class E. It is still bearing SR style numbers more than five years after nationalisation, although displaying a BR number. (N.W.Sprinks)

95. Occasional railtours have visited the branch. This is the RCTS "Invicta" on 12th September 1954, headed by class R1 0-4-4T no.31671. The tour commenced at Liverpool Street and ran via the East London Line, Blackheath and Woolwich. It continued through Faversham, Canterbury Spur, Minster, Deal and Kearsney to Ashford, where there was a visit to the shed and works. Return was by way of Tonbridge, Oxted, the Mid-Kent Line and Peckham Rye, finishing at Blackfriars. (F.Hornby)

96. The timber framed and clad building was an economical form of construction and was of a design widely used by the SER but less so by the LCDR. Practicality had superseded flamboyance in this example of railway architecture. (British Rail)

97. Following the lengthening of platform 1, the starting signal (left) was moved 107yds southwards on 23rd March 1938. No. 1 was then 271yds, and no.2 137 yds, in length. Seen in May 1956, the signal box remained in use until 24th May 1959. (J.J.Smith)

98. With spare coaches in the sidings, BR class 2 2-6-2T no.41308 is ready with the 12.12pm to Chatham while C class 0-6-0 no.31682 waits with the 1.5pm to Sittingbourne on 22nd June 1957. Only the centre track had been replaced with flat-bottom rail by then. (J.H.Aston)

99. The duo seen in picture 88 have plenty of steam ready to depart at 6.50pm with the return excursion to Victoria on 25th May 1958. Although not listed as a goods station, coal was unloaded here by the Co-operative Wholesale Society. (S.C.Nash)

100. In March 1971 a train collided with the buffers, demolished half the station, killed one passenger and injured several others. This is the scene on 15th July 1972 as reconstruction was in progress and a Morris Oxford waits for passengers. (Dr.E.Course)

101. Surprisingly all three lines were electrified in 1959 but one crossover was removed later. It was probably anticipated that electric locomotives might be used on excursion trains. A class 411/5 unit is at platform 1 on 5th July 1992, platform 2 seldom being used. (F.Hornby)

102. Seen in September 1992, the station was well sited, being at the end of the High Street, adjacent to the bus station and close to the beach. Although a ticket machine is in place, the booking office was still staffed on weekday mornings. (J.Scrace)

4. Sheppey Light Railway

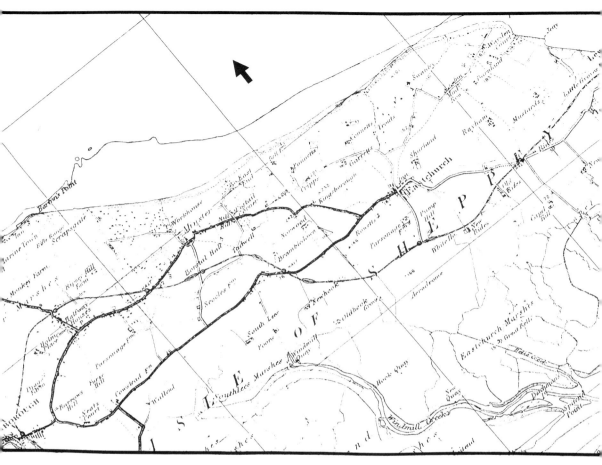

XVIII.   Conceived by local landowners, the scheme soon came to the notice of a young railway engineer, Holman F. Stephens, later to become well known as Colonel Stephens and for his involvement in minor railways throughout Britain. Prior to this, he had been resident engineer on the Cranbrook & Paddock Wood Railway (see our *Branch Line to Hawkhurst*) and had subsequently established a civil engineering practice in Tonbridge. He was thus well placed and experienced to survey and construct a line to Leysdown. This was one of his first three major projects, the others being lines to Tenterden and Selsey. Unlike the Hawkhurst branch, it was built under the 1896 Light Railways Act which allowed for simplified signalling, minimal passenger facilities, and lightweight rail but imposed limits on axle weight and speed, in this case the latter being 25mph.

The map of 1921 at 1" to 1 mile shows the full length of the branch which was almost nine miles. The population of Eastchurch was 1141 at this time, having risen from 784 when the line opened. The comparable figures for Leysdown were 222 and 221, having dipped to 151 at the 1911 census.

Sheppey Light Railway.—The Sheppey Light Railway is a Single Line, with Run-Round Loops at Queenboro', Eastchurch and Leysdown, and is worked on the Train Staff and Ticket System, as under :—

BETWEEN.	DESCRIPITON OF TRAIN STAFF.	COLOUR OF TRAIN TICKET.
Queenboro' and Eastchurch..	Round Brass Bar	Yellow.
Eastchurch and Leysdown	Round Brass Bar	Pink.

These Train Staffs are necessary to unlock the Siding Points at the various Stations and Sidings, and any Train having work to do at any of the Sidings must always have the proper Train Staff.

No Engine, Carriage, Wagon or other Vehicle (whether Loaded or Empty) the weight of which exceeds **14 Tons** on any pair of Wheels must be used on this Light Railway, with the exception of the Ballast Engine now in use.

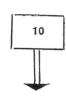

Speed.—The **maximum** speed allowed for any Train or Engine is 25 miles per hour. If a Tender Engine is used and is run Tender first the speed must not exceed 15 miles per hour.

Speed must be reduced at all Level Crossings and Sharp Curves to 10 miles per hour, and Warning Boards are provided, painted White with a large **10** in Black, at all such points. At the Accommodation or Farm Crossings, where no Gates are provided, Cattle Guards are put down. At all such Level Crossings where Gates are not erected and maintained across the Railway, the speed must be reduced to **10** miles an hour **for the distance of 300 yards approaching the Crossing.** Enginemen must sound the Whistle when approaching **all** Crossings. No Engine, Train or Vehicle must be allowed to stand foul of any public road over which the Railway may cross.

Gate Crossings.—Public Road Crossings exist at Sheerness East Station, East Minster-on-Sea (about midway between Sheerness East and Minster), Minster Station, Lower Road (between Minster and Eastchurch), Eastchurch Station, Harty Road (between Eastchurch and Leysdown).

In addition to the above, numerous Farm and Accommodation Crossings exist, some of which are provided with Gates, and others with Cattle Guards but no Gates.

Farmers' Sidings.—Farmers' Sidings are provided as follows :—Brambledown Siding (about ¾-mile on the Eastchurch side of Minster Station), Grove Siding (about 1 mile beyond Brambledown Siding and nearer to Eastchurch), Holford Siding (about 1 mile beyond Eastchurch, between Eastchurch and Harty Road Gate Crossing), Harty Road Siding (close to the Gate Crossing at this point). All these Sidings, as well as the Sidings at Leysdown, Eastchurch, Minster and Sheerness East, are on the **UP** side of the Line.

These Sidings are located under the various Stations as follows :—

> Brambledown Siding ⎤
> Grove   ,, ⎬ under Eastchurch.
> Holford   ,, ⎦
> Harty Road   ,,   ,, Leysdown.

Running Round Trains at Queenboro', Eastchurch and Leysdown.—Care must be taken to keep Engines and Vehicles clear of the Catch Points provided in these Run-round Loops until the same have been properly set for passing over them.

Passenger Traffic is only booked locally from and to Queenboro'.

Minster Station on this Railway must always be referred to as **Minster-on-Sea** in all entries re Goods, Parcels, &c., as a distinction from Minster Junction (Thanet).

All Correspondence, Invoices, &c., for any of the Stations on this Light Railway to be addressed to the Station Master at Queenboro'.

SECR Appendix for 1922

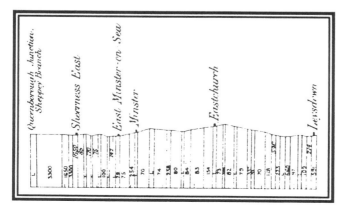

QUEENBOROUGH

103.   Standing in the branch bay on 19th September 1947 is a new van coupled to an old locomotive, class R no.1667 built for the LCDR by Sharp Stewart in 1891. Engines past their prime were the norm on the line, the exception being P class 0-6-0Ts which were introduced around 1910. (J.H.Aston)

104.   Waiting by the water column in 1949 is another R class, no.1673. The 14-chain curve in the background was the sharpest on the branch. Note that through running from the main line was not possible.
(Dr.P.Ransome Wallis/NRM)

105. The last day of operation was Saturday 2nd December 1950 and the inevitable band of photographers was in attendance. No.31705 was a class R1 0-4-4T, built by Sharp Stewart in 1900. The run-round loop was beyond the curve. (Pamlin Prints)

SHEERNESS EAST

↑

Race Course

Road

Tramway
Depôt

50
63

Sheerness East
Station

Cattle Pens

Electric Po
Station

CATHERINE ROAD

106. Two short sidings diverge from the headshunt, an arrangement that changed little over the years. Look for the tramway standard and the recently arrived cable drum, and also note Stephens' economical timber platform edging, soon replaced here and elsewhere by more durable material. (D.Miles coll.)

XIX. The 1908 survey includes the terminus and depot of the 3ft 6ins gauge 2½ mile long Sheerness Tramway which was in use from 9th April 1903 until 7th July 1917. Prior to WWI crowds of Sheerness residents would make day trips to the beach at Leysdown by tram and train, changing here. Had the tramway been allowed to cross the railway, and had the railway run to Sheerness, both ventures might have been more successful. The power station of the Sheerness & District Electrical Power & Traction Co. Ltd. is marked. Note the proximity of the race course which may have generated some railway revenue.

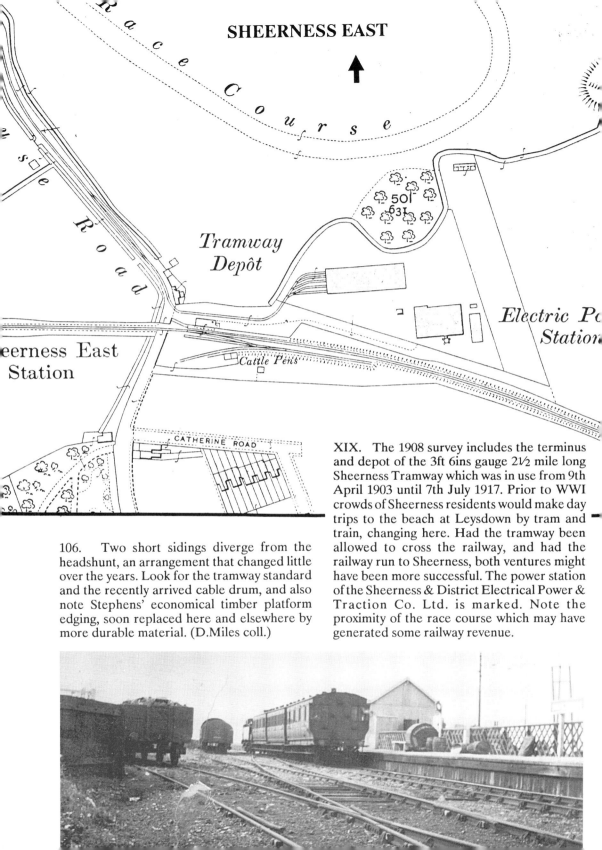

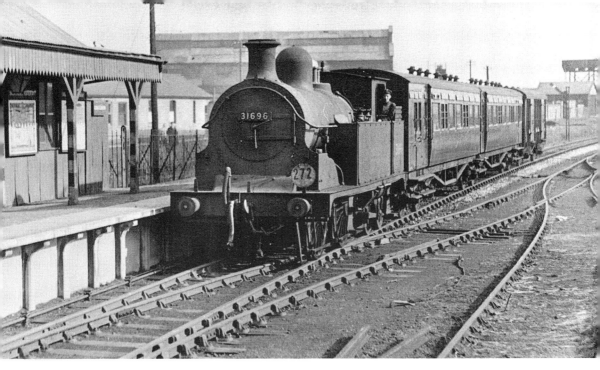

107.   Steam powered railcars were tried in 1905-07 but were not popular. Their bodies were eventually paired up onto a common bogie and subsequently served the line well for about forty years. One pair is seen behind class R1 no.31696 which is obscuring the power station. This was diesel operated in its latter years. (Dr.P.Ransome Wallis/NRM)

108.   The building is typical of those specified by Stephens for most of the lines for which he was engineer. Examples survive in Kent at Bodiam and Northiam but no trace remains of the Sheppey Light Railway, except the platform facing seen here. The station was a block post but the two signals were not added until 24th April 1945. Stephens sometimes provided facilities for gentlemen but not for ladies. (S.C.Nash)

EAST MINSTER-ON-SEA

109. Like the platform edging, Stephens' wooden fencing was of limited life expectancy and was soon replaced by less attractive iron railings. It appears that the platform face was replaced by brick but extended in timber, as shown in the next picture. (D.Miles coll.)

XX. The 1908 map shows little housing development and the original station name. More accurate would have been "West Minster" but there is a place of this name between Queenborough and Sheerness as well as the world famous one.

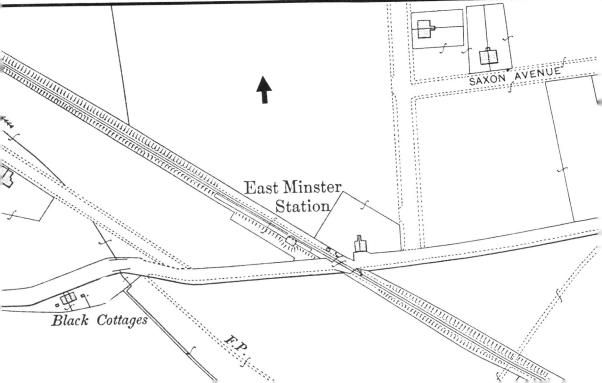

SAXON AVENUE

East Minster Station

Black Cottages

F.P.

110. Some residential building took place but lack of a direct rail service to Sheerness was a passenger deterrent. Initially the halt was used "only on specified occasions" but was brought into regular use in 1902. (Pamlin Prints)

This footplate pass was issued to W.H. Austen, assistant to the engineer of the line, H.F.Stephens. It was initialled in red by Mr.Wainwright. (Colonel Stephens Railway Archive)

6242

SOUTHERN RAILWAY.
Issued subject to the Bye-laws, Regulations & Conditions in the Company's Bills and Notices.

RAIL MOTOR CAR.

NOT TRANSFERABLE
To be shown on demand.

THIRD CLASS SINGLE
Fare 11d.

BETWEEN

Brambledown Halt &
LEYSDOWN

The Passenger is requested to see this ticket punched at the time of issue.

5482

SOUTHERN RAILWAY.
Issued subject to the Bye-laws, Regulations & Conditions in the Company's Bills and Notices.

RAIL MOTOR CAR.

NOT TRANSFERABLE
To be shown on demand.

THIRD CLASS SINGLE
Fare 4½d.

BETWEEN

Sheerness East &
MINSTER-ON-SEA

East Minster-on-Sea &
BRAMBLEDOWN HALT

Brambledown Halt &
EASTCHURCH

Harty Road Halt &
LEYSDOWN

The Passenger is requested to see this ticket punched at the time of issue.

SOUTH EASTERN AND CHATHAM RAILWAY.

LOCOMOTIVE DEPARTMENT,
ASHFORD KENT.

No. 63   7th August 1901

ENGINE PASS.

Pass Mr. Inspector W Austen

on the Engine between

Queenborough

and   Leysdown

In force until the 31st December 1901

for Harry S. Wainwright

EnP   Locomotive Engineer

This Engine Pass is issued upon the understanding that it will only be used when absolutely necessary for the purpose of inspecting the Line or Engine, or in the performance of similar responsibility.
To be shown to the Inspector when required.
To be returned to the Locomotive Engineer's Office immediately after date of expiry.

(See Conditions on back.)

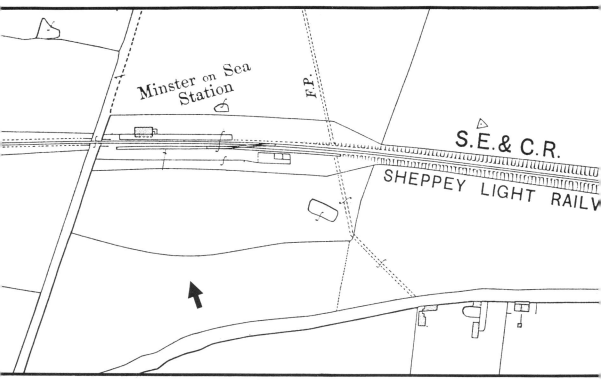

XXI.   The 1908 map shows the name in use from June 1907. Previously having been Minster (Sheppey), there was a risk of confusion with Minster in Thanet. The town grew from 1600 in 1901 to 3700 in 1936 but bus services were more convenient for most people after WWI.

111.   Always a block post, signals were added on 24th April 1945, these being controlled from two levers in the booking office. A similar ground frame at the east end of the platform was provided for the points, the frame being unlocked by the train staff key. (D.Cullum)

BRAMBLEDOWN HALT

112. This stopping place was added in March 1905 when the steam railcars were introduced. Their bodies (two of which are illustrated here) rested on the engine frame and in consequence suffered considerable vibration. Class R1 no.31696 and the gated siding are seen in 1950. (Dr.P.Ransome-Wallis/NRM)

XXII. Only described as a siding on the 1908 survey, the halt was named after the nearest farm to the north. The road at the level crossing is now the A250 to Leysdown.

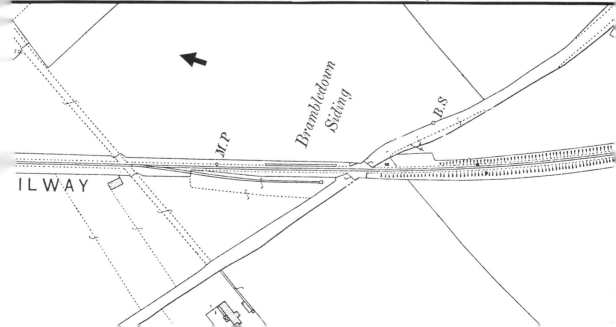

EASTCHURCH

113.   This was the main station on the route and the terminus of winter services for the first few years. The passing loop was not used for the passing of passenger trains.
(Lens of Sutton)

XXIII.   The 1908 edition includes the cattle market which was opened in February 1902 and which would have generated additional railway revenue. The local population was only 900 in 1901.

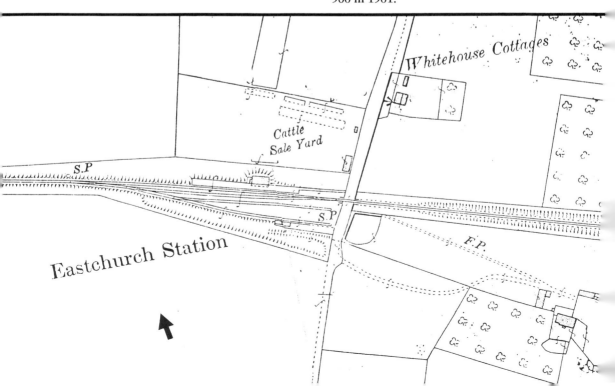

114.   The Royal Naval Aviation School was opened on the high ground south of the station in 1916. It became an RAF station and by 1936 accommodated over 1000 personnel, which gave rise to considerable passenger peaks on the line and often heavy freight traffic. A siding facing Queenborough came off the main line to serve the camp. (Pamlin Prints)

115.   Four track workers were injured in August 1940 when enemy aircraft missed their target, the RAF establishment. Class R1 no.31698 is working the 11.36am from Leysdown on 21st October 1950 and is passing the down signal which is "off". Since the introduction of long-token working on 18th January 1930 for the entire branch, all intermediate signals could be left in this position. The small arm was for the goods loop. (J.J.Smith)

HARTY ROAD HALT

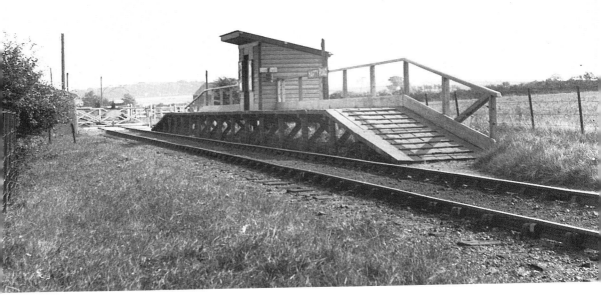

116. It is difficult to imagine why a halt was opened in March 1905 at this desolate location, two miles from the few houses on the Isle of Harty. Additional agricultural sidings were provided both sides of Eastchurch - Grove Siding to the west and Holford Siding to the east, both on the south side and facing Queenborough. The standard structure was provided but later an enormous green enamelled signboard was erected, almost as big as the shelter. The guard was obliged to open the gates over the A250. Trains stopped here and at Brambledown Halt during daylight hours only, although special arrangements could be made for passengers to use the halts during darkness at their own risk.
(Lens of Sutton)

1906

SHEPPEY LIGHT RAILWAY.

	Down.	Week Days.						Sundays.		
Miles		mrn	mrn	mrn	aft	aft	Tues. & Sats.	aft	mrn	aft
	Queenboro'...............dep.	7	0	9	5	11 0	12 45	3 30	6 30	11 35	6 30
1	Sheerness East	7	5	9 10	11 5	12 45	3 35	6 35	11 40	6 35
1½	East Minster-on-Sea	Sig.	Sig.	Sig.	Sig.	Sig.	Sig.		Sig.	Sig.
2½	Minster (Sheppey)	7 12	9 17	11 12	12 52	3 42	6 42		11 47	6 42
3	Eastchurch	7 20	9 25	11 20	1 0	2 50		6 50		11 55	6 50
4	Leysdown ....arr.			9s35	11s30	1 10	4 0		7 0		12 5

s Saturdays only.

1908 map

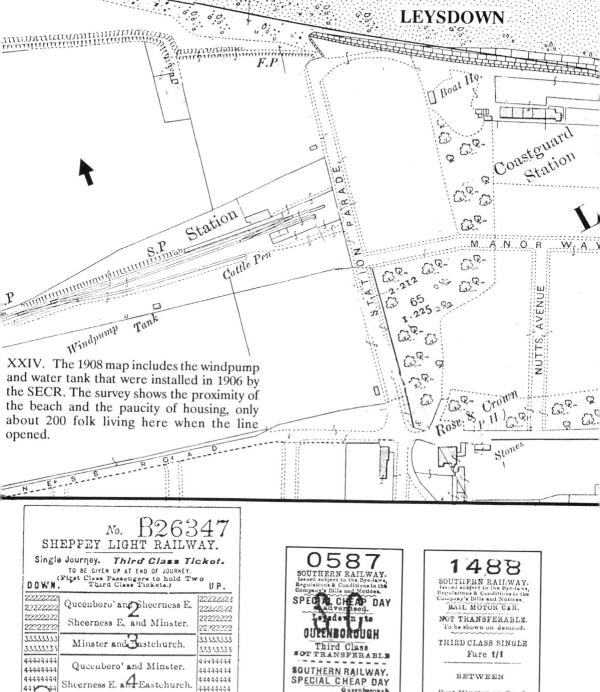

LEYSDOWN

XXIV. The 1908 map includes the windpump and water tank that were installed in 1906 by the SECR. The survey shows the proximity of the beach and the paucity of housing, only about 200 folk living here when the line opened.

No. **B26347**

SHEPPEY LIGHT RAILWAY.

Single Journey.   *Third Class Ticket.*
TO BE GIVEN UP AT END OF JOURNEY.
(First Class Passengers to hold Two
Third Class Tickets.)

DOWN.		UP.
22222222	Queenboro' and Sheerness E.	22222222
	Sheerness E. and Minster. 2	
33333333	Minster and Eastchurch. 3	33333333
44444444	Queenboro' and Minster.	44444444
	Sheerness E. and Eastchurch. 4	
	Eastchurch and Leysdown.	
66666666	Queenboro' and Eastchurch.	66666666
	Minster and Leysdown. 6	
77777777	Sheerness E. and Leysdown. 7	77777777
99999999	Queenboro' and Leysdown. 9	99999999
66666666	Excess Luggage, &c. 6	66666666

0587
SOUTHERN RAILWAY.
Issued subject to the Bye-laws,
Regulations & Conditions in the
Company's Bills and Notices.
SPECIAL CHEAP DAY
as advertised.
Leysdown to
QUEENBOROUGH
Third Class
NOT TRANSFERABLE
- - - - - - - - - - - - -
SOUTHERN RAILWAY.
SPECIAL CHEAP DAY
Queenborough
Leysdown
Queenborough   to
LEYSDOWN
Third Class
0587

1488
SOUTHERN RAILWAY.
Issued subject to the Bye-laws,
Regulations & Conditions in the
Company's Bills and Notices.
RAIL MOTOR CAR.
NOT TRANSFERABLE.
To be shown on demand.

THIRD CLASS SINGLE
Fare 1/1

BETWEEN

East Minster-on-Sea &

LEYSDOWN

The Passenger is requested to see
this ticket punched at the time
of issue.

SHEPPEY LIGHT RAILWAY STATION, LEYSDOWN

117. An early postcard view has the front of the station partially obscured by the cattle pens, which were probably of more importance for revenue. The lack of windpump suggests that the picture was taken during the first five years of operation. (Lens of Sutton)

118. The bunker seems well filled as ex-SER Q class no.73 waits to return to Queenborough with its train of six-wheelers. The braziers would have been required by the water column in the freezing east winds that blew up the platform at this exposed location. (Lens of Sutton)

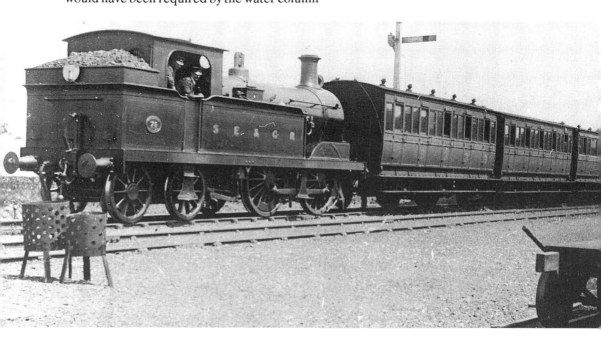

119. A 1949 photograph from the cattle dock shows class R 0-4-4T no.1673 running round its train. Only for a few years was push-pull working employed on the branch. As at Eastchurch, only gentlemen could make themselves comfortable on the premises. A six-lever ground frame was provided at the far end of the station.
(Dr.P.Ransome Wallis/NRM)

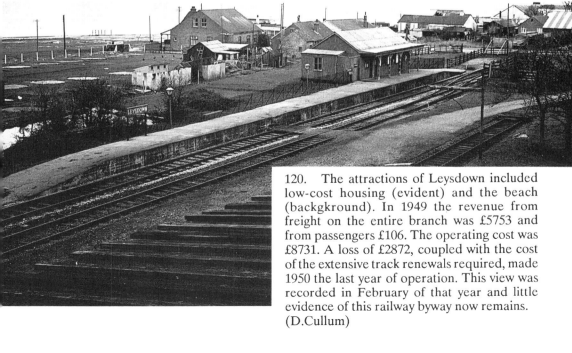

120.   The attractions of Leysdown included low-cost housing (evident) and the beach (backgkround). In 1949 the revenue from freight on the entire branch was £5753 and from passengers £106. The operating cost was £8731. A loss of £2872, coupled with the cost of the extensive track renewals required, made 1950 the last year of operation. This view was recorded in February of that year and little evidence of this railway byway now remains.
(D.Cullum)